W9-BUW-535

A Seventy-Fifth Anniversary Snap Shot
(1975-2000): One Supervisor's View

TABLE OF CONTENTS

99387

ACKNOWLEDGEMENTS

These "snap shots" are a retired supervisor's reflections on the past 58 years, aided by input from many persons. Some will be identified in the text, but a sincere "thank you" also goes to those who were not listed. I want to pay special tribute to these unnamed supervisors, seminary and denominational representatives who have enabled ACPE to continue growing during these years. We need a complete list of all who have served on the various regional and national governance portions of ACPE. We also remember those whose vision, planning and hard work have made possible both the regional and Annual ACPE conferences. These meetings have been times for the renewal of friendships, making new friendships and furthering our continuing education.

We say a special "thank you" to those in positions of regional leadership who have kept the regions relevant, vital and alive in the midst of so many external demands on time and energy. The writer apologizes to all those whose contributions made the story possible but who are unnamed. A review of the history reveals so many persons not mentioned here by name but without whose presence the ACPE would not have survived to be as vigorous as it is today.

A grateful debt is owed to the 1999 history network of regional history representatives who birthed the need for such a history. Homer Jernigan and Robert Leas have given many hours and ideas, and served as the editorial committee supporting this project, but are not responsible for its content. In addition, Duane Parker, Max Maguire, Keith Keidel, Bill Baugh, Dan DeArment, Robert Powell, and Jerry Davis have given helpful suggestions to recent drafts of the text, but are likewise not responsible for its content. Many others have read sections of the text appropriate to their areas of experience and expertise and have made helpful suggestions. The list of these people would be very lengthy. Each one deserves to be listed by name, but that is not possible. Each of them has been thanked. Sincere apologies are given for the omission of their names.

Gratitude is given to the members of the Retired Supervisors' Network who in their 1999 meeting, also in Albuquerque, endorsed the History Project. More than fifty of their members funded this project with nearly $6,500.00 in gifts between $25.00 and $1,500.00, as did the Northeast, Eastern, North Central and South Central Regions. (See Appendix VII for list of donors.)

We thank the many that have contributed to this work to make it more accurate so that its pages represent the present status of ACPE. We also thank those who have given permission to reprint quotations from their words in e mail messages, journals and books.

Finally, for those whose technical support have made this effort possible: to Bill Detra, computer "guru" who has "saved" the text many times; for Chris McCreary, editor and MSS preparer for her energetic and timely support; and to the church office staff, including Mick Horn and Deb Furlong. Special appreciation is extended to Dr. Jonathan Smoot, Senior Pastor; the Session and its Personnel Committee of Christ Presbyterian Church, Madison, Wisconsin, who made possible the sabbatical and vacation time available so this volume could meet the 75th Anniversary deadline. A thankful appreciation is given to the late Marguerite Thomas for her support over 27 years,. A final deep "thank you" to Margaret Thomas, whose support these past 26 years made this all possible; her "red pencil" proof-reading of many rough drafts of the text made this final text a reality.

PREFACE

This is a "snap shot" of CPE history, and a limited one at that. It is not a supervisor's memoirs nor a professional historian's presentation.

Sources include the many ACPE reports, papers, minutes, journals and reference books at the author's home, including nearly every copy of the News published between 1967 and 2000 by the Association for Clinical Pastoral Education, Inc. (ACPE). Sources also include personal papers, reflections of past presidents both written and on videotape, and various editions of the ACPE Constitution and By-laws.

We are greatly indebted to medical historian and physician, Robert C. Powell, for his scholarly work, *Fifty Years of Learning, Through Supervised Encounter With Living Human Documents, (ACPE, 1975)* covering the first fifty years. Hopefully, someone might do that for these past twenty-five (25) years. Complete access is needed to the complete sets of Minutes of the Annual Meetings, the meetings of House of Delegates and its executive Committees, the General Assembly and its Board of Represen- tatives, the Annual Meetings and its Board of Representatives since 1992 to accomplish that task. Minutes of the Meetings of the Commissions, Committees, Task Forces, Special Study Committees and the Networks will also be necessary, as well as the audited Annual Financial Reports, all of which are available at the ACPE Office in Decatur, GA. We thank our interim Office Manager, Nancy Parker, for organizing and making this material available for such a purpose. Unfortunately, this writer did not have either the time or the funds to carefully review many of these materials in the ACPE office nor those at the ACPE archives at the Pitts Theology Library, Emory University, Atlanta.

There is an excellent collection of videotapes of some of the pioneers, initiated by the then History Chairs Keith Keidel, Tom Cole, Ralph Carpenter and others in the late 1970's. George Colgin expanded these in the later 1980's. A new program of taping Supervisors Emeritus at the annual meetings and other locations has resulted in oral history tapes of some fifty , mostly retired supervisors, their lives and their ministries.

This "snap shot" view of CPE history comes from a retired certified supervisor with fifty-two years of involvement as a supervisor in the movement. After three units of CPE with the Council for Clinical Training (CCT) in 1942 (Donald Beatty),

1943 (Fred Kuether), and 1946 (William Andrew); a summer of very part-time in 1944 (Russell Dicks); and eighteen months of active duty as a Naval Reserve Chaplain, this writer began supervision at Cook County Hospital, Chicago, in 1948 and was certified in 1949. This writer's professional experience included ministry as hospital chaplain and supervisor in Illinois, Texas and Wisconsin for thirty years (ten years in general hospitals and twenty years in psychiatric hospitals), three more years on active duty (1950-1953) and five years on a seminary faculty (part-time, 1957-1962). Since retirement in 1980 the parish has been the locale of ministry (1981-).

Limited writings in addition to some journal articles include: *A New Approach To The Doctrine of Man* (1944), BD Thesis, McCormick Theological Seminary, Chicago, IL; *A Survey of the Interpretations of And Attitudes Toward Illness in A Series of Cancer Patients* (1550), MA Thesis, Garrett Biblical Institute-Northwestern University, Evanston, IL; A *Manual for Naval Hospital Chaplains* (NAVPERS 15995) (1974), Washington, DC; "The Chaplain As A Member Of The Psychiatric Team" (July, 1967), in Hospital and Community Psychiatry, John R. Thomas and Leonard I. Stein, M.D.; "Marguerite and Me" (Fall-Winter 1972), in Pilgrimage, A Journal of Pastoral Psychotherapy; "Me-Without Marguerite" (Winter-Spring, 1975), in Pilgrimage; "A Comparative Evaluation in Changes in Basic CPE Students in Different Types of Clinical Settings" (September 1982), John R. Thomas, Leonard I. Stein, M.D. and Marjorie Klein, Ph.D., Journal of Pastoral Care, Vol. XXXVI, No. 3; *A Brief History of the North Central Region of ACPE, Inc. 1967-1987* (1987, 1996 Revision), North Central Region Office; and "The College of Chaplains: Some Historical Perspectives: 1971-1995" (1996), The Caregiver Journal, Vol. 12 No. 1, College of Chaplains (now APC), Schaumburg, IL.

Regional activities and national responsibilities have been extensive during chaplaincy years and since, giving this writer an inside picture of many of these years. He served as the North Central Region's Director, 1966-1979; President-elect; President; Past President, ACPE (1979-1982); and one of the ex-officio members of the Special Study Committee (1978-1980). He then served as a member and then Chair of the History Committee prior to serving as History Coordinator, 1992-present. This writer was proud to receive the ACPE's Distinguished Service Award in 1988, as well as to receive awards from The Association of Mental Health Clergy, the College of Chaplains, Carroll College and the John Park Lee

Award of the Presbyterian Health, Education and Welfare Association. These awards are one of the advantages of living a long life!

INTRODUCTION – CPE, WHAT IS IT?

Many reading this account have had some CPE experience and hopefully have known personally at first hand the "ah-ha" transforming moment or have experienced a rebirth in either or both of the religious and psychological arenas of life. This CPE experience started out in the Protestant Christian tradition. Later on, it included the Roman Catholic tradition and, in very recent years, the Jewish, Muslim and Buddhist communities. In CPE, one begins to understand one's self in terms of motivations and one's patterns of human relationships, and thus is given a new understanding of one's "call " to ministry and one's relationship with The Transcendent. This religious and psychological enrichment has taken place primarily within the context of the Christian tradition. The spouse who was not in the training program sometimes found it difficult to understand this transformation.

A couple of examples will attempt to give those with no ACPE experience a "feel" for these "head and heart" turning points. (2, 3, 4). Listen to how an early student reported on his transforming experience: (Student A. 1951. JPC. p. 33.)

> In our seminars, I found a greater degree of love than I had previously known. Here was a group who watched me grow angry and withdraw, which listened to me tell them they didn't know what they were talking about, which discovered the really basic flaws and weaknesses in my personality – and none of these things made any difference in our relationships. I was still liked and kept as a welcome member of the group. Of course, this was a gradual process. But as time passed, I saw ever more clearly that I didn't have to do anything special to win their favor. I did not have to agree with their opinions. I did not have to pretend I was always right. I did not even have to be pleasant. No matter what I did, or how I acted, or what they found out about me, they did not exclude me from the fellowship. They accepted me just as I was. It was as simple as that.

Listen to some students reporting their experiences within the past two years:

This eleven-week unit has been the most powerful learning and spiritually growthful time of my life. I have seen illness and death and grief up close and personal, really for the first time in my life, and it has impacted on me personally, spiritually, theologically & inter-personally. I have had four amazing peer teachers and four powerful supervisor teachers leading me and showing me the way while helping me and encouraging me to find my own way. I have examined my ministry, my personality, my priorities, my biases and prejudices, my strengths and my weaknesses. And I have opened some doors of darkness, and found light where fear lived, but I have walked by some others, too scary to open, or, in some cases, to even acknowledge.

Another student focused on the ministry aspects of the CPE experience:

I've made significant progress in using prayer with people, both in terms of having a store of traditional prayers as a base and in terms of more spontaneous prayer. I have come to appreciate the value of this pastoral tool... I've learned spiritual assessments can be helpful, particularly in initiating significant conversations. I also appreciate that having a pastoral plan is helpful and consistent with lack of agenda. I've made progress in being more assertive on behalf of the persons I care for... I've made progress in sensitivity to my own limits and the need to set boundaries.

Still another student reported:

I am realizing that it has been one of the most significant experiences I have had in my life. When I found myself grieving the ending, these words crossed my mind: these people, this program, the experience will always be with you, you take it with you on your journey. It has been a blessing, of learning to "be" in ministry... In all this I find myself listening to God/dess. The more I am open to this experience, the more beautiful the experience becomes. I have found encouragement here to continue to use ritual, bodywork, breathing and many unusual ways of assisting/enhancing my listening as well as my worship.

BRIEF HISTORY

The early history can be found in Robert Powell's book, *CPE Fifty Years of Learning, Through Supervised Encounter With Living Human Documents* (ACPE); in Edward Thornton's *Professional Education for Ministry* (1970), Abingdon; and Charles E. Hall's *Head and Heart, The Story of Clinical Pastoral Education* (1991), Journal of Pastoral Care Publications, Decatur, GA (especially chapters 7, 8 and 9).

Additional resources are:

Asquith, Glen H. Jr., Editor. (1992). *Vision From A Little Known Country, A Boisen Reader.* Journal of Care Publications. Decatur, GA.
Buford, Paula. (1997). *The Lost Tradition of Women Pastoral Caregivers from 1925-1967: A 'Dangerous Memory'* (Th.D. Thesis). Columbia Theological Seminary. Decatur, GA
Hemenway, Joan A. (1996). *Inside the Circle, A Historical and Practical Inquiry Concerning Process Groups in Clinical Pastoral Education.* Journal of Pastoral Care Publications. Decatur, GA.
Holifield, E. Brooks. (1970). <u>A History of Pastoral Care in America, From Salvation to Self-Realization.</u> Abingdon Press: Nashville, TN.
Stokes, Allison. (1985). <u>Ministry After Freud.</u> Pilgrim Press: New York, NY.

We are celebrating 75 years of CPE, but only 33 years as ACPE. Prior organization's histories go back to 1930 –the Council for Clinical Training (CCT)– and to 1944 –the Institute for Pastoral Care (IPC).

The CPE centers supervisors, seminary members and some denominations have created a CPE movement which reaches back to 1925, while ACPE as an organization dates back to 1967, when the merger of four predecessor organizations took place. The story begins with Rev. Anton T. Boisen's psychotic break at the age of 45. He was hospitalized from October 20, 1920, at the Westboro State Hospital until January, 1922. Afterwards, as a special student at Andover Theological Seminary, he took courses with Dr. Richard Cabot and other professors in the fields of psychology and psychiatry. Dr. Boisen had been employed as Chaplain at the Worcester State Hospital, Worcester, Massachusetts in 1924 by Dr.William A. Bryan, the Worcester Superintendent. Dr. Bryan, criticized for hiring a chaplain, responded: "I would employ a horse doctor if it made my patients get better." Anton T. Boisen accepted four theological students at the hospital in the summer of 1925 for what was first called "clinical training."

Who could have imagined that the humble beginning in 1925 would grow to an organization today which presently consists of over 340 centers, 670 supervisors, 126 supervisory candidates, 117 member seminaries and 663 clinical members? (ACPE office report, Feb. 15, 2000.)

> The ACPE mission is to foster experience-based theological education that combines the practice of pastoral care with qualified supervision and peer group reflection and which is grounded in a person-centered approach to religious ministry (adopted in 1980). (This mission statement is currently under review.)

Men and, much later, women, who cared about understanding their religious faith in relation to human problems, produced this movement. They wanted to improve the training of the clergy for ministry to troubled people. Because it had been a rebirth or transforming experience for them, they wanted to pass this opportunity on to others. One of its other sources was a rebellion against the rigid norms and mores of traditional religions and religious practices.

Early supervisors in both of the two first training groups: The Council for Clinical Training, Inc. (1930) and the Institute for Pastoral Care, Inc. (1944) wanted to change theological education to incorporate "clinical training." They were all men, all Protestant, all white and all seminary graduates. It was not until 1948 that the first African-American man, Merrel Booker, was certified. It was not until 1949 that a female certified Supervisor, Louise Long, attended a CCT Fall conference. The charge was valid that it was "an old boys network" even though the "boys" were in their 30's and 40's.

The CCT Supervisors talked about belonging to the "fellowship of sinners" as one way of accepting the human condition and identifying themselves. Listening and being vulnerable was one way of relating to hurting people, whether one's parishioners were in a state mental hospital, a reformatory, a general hospital or a parish church. Their primary accountability was to the superintendent of a hospital or the warden of a prison and they were remotely accountable to religious authorities. They had to learn the institution's hierarchies of power. While the early general hospital chaplaincy positions were more often in religious institutions, increasingly the movement of chaplaincy and CPE entered the governmental and non-profit institutions. Some denominations were quite supportive of their clergy who moved into the chaplaincy and CPE, granting scholarships for CPE training to local pastors and seminary students. In other denominations, chaplains and pastoral counselors had to organize themselves and lobby for the right to be heard within the denomination and its agencies. Among the major denominations, the Methodists, Lutherans, and Baptists took a more supportive role with their chaplains and pastoral counselors.

Denominational approval was not always automatic simply because one was listed in the official clergy roster. A few denominations even started requiring some CPE prior to endorsing their clergy to chaplaincy positions in institutions.

Nearly all ACPE supervisors have had to function on the boundaries with the resulting tensions and, in the earlier years, at a significant personal and family financial handicap. Yet, they persevered in this ministry so that CPE became an acceptable part of theological education for some denominations. Not only did they persevere but they spread the CPE story to hospitals and other settings in developing new programs and enlisting new seminary members to join ACPE. They also spread the good news of CPE to a wide variety of other countries.

The goals of this process-focused education are two-fold: first, to develop one's pastoral care skills, and second, to increase one's self-understanding. Most of the seminary students, clergy, religious and laity that complete the program (various units in length) achieve such benefits. CPE also provides continuing education for clergy who desire to move into full-time chaplaincy positions and supervisory certification.

SOME PERSECTIVES AND RESOURCES FROM THE PAST

Some "snap shots" from people both inside and outside of CPE follow. Robert Powell, in his address to the 50th Anniversary Conference of CPE, raised several questions. The first one was *Should CPE have any role in training the laity, especially physicians, in some aspects of pastoral care?* (ACPE Conference Proceedings. 1975. p. 13.)

He went on to pose an additional series of questions:

> Let me repeat, once more my Bosien-esque questions from the past, and with them, end. <u>Whatever happened to pastoral social work? to religious diagnosis? to preventive pastoral care? To maintenance, everyday, pastoral care? To the theology of pastoral care</u> —especially the theology of everyday life? <u>Whatever happened to religious rituals and symbolism? to religious research? to the development of a critical tradition within CPE?</u> As a historian I can pose these eight questions from the past, but you as CPE educators, must provide the current contexts and answers. (p. 14.)

Before we answer some of these questions, let us get some historical perspective on the antecedents of CPE. This will help us in our understanding of CPE to learn about where we came from. Some articles in the 1975 Fiftieth Anniversary Edition of the Journal of Pastoral Care (June, 1975. Vol. XXIX, NO. 2), will give some historical perspective. First, let us listen to historian Hugh B. Hammett:

> We have seen that the movement for clinical pastoral education in the 1920's may be viewed as a response to the menacing, multi-headed hydra of technology, capitalism, urbanization and industrialism. Clinical pastoral education, however, was not just a reaction to new conditions. It may be properly seen as a building-on or a continuation of earlier, related reform concerns. (7, 82)

Hammett goes on to relate CPE to the mission of the church:

> The mission of the Church, by this view, was to Christianize the environment in which humans lived and worked. (p. 83.)

From this perspective:

> Clinical pastoral education, then, was a continuation of a past tradition of bettering. The concern of CPE was more individual and personal than societal. The movement was a search for ways of effective ministry to individuals under the stresses of all that modern life demands. (p. 84-85.)

Walter Rauschenbush, pioneer in Social Gospel, said:

> Saving the human race was as important as saving the human soul... It is the function of religion to teach the individual to value his soul more than his body. (Rauschenbush. 1907. p. 367-372.)

Jenny Yates Hammett, a philosopher, points out:

> However, as liberalism and progressivism waned, clinical pastoral education was just beginning to be established as a movement, embodying emphasis on scientific method... Only indirectly do we see the influence of the emerging neo-orthodoxy on the development of the clinical pastoral education movement. In the late 1930's and early 1940's, CPE defined the split between the views of Robert E. Brinkman and Seward Hiltner. The Brinkman school emphasized science subsuming theology while the Hiltner tradition stressed theological thinking about human experience... Although CPE went through the era of a developing neo-orthodoxy and a developing existentialism, it appears not to have changed its basic liberal orientation of scientific method over theological content. (Hammett. 1975. JPC. p. 88-89.)

She concludes her review:

> Perhaps now is the time in a fifty year retrospect to imbibe a retrieving and renewing theological drink. (p. 89)

In 1953, an early leader, Frederick C. Kuether had posed the three questions in chronological order which supervisors had asked, "What must I do to help? What must I know to help? What can I say to help?" (Pastoral Psychology. Vol. 4, No. 37. p. 19-20.) The fourth question, which by then the supervisors and the students were asking, was:

> What must I *be* to be of help to the patient? Because I bring myself to every human encounter, I must understand and accept myself. Until I do this, I cannot understand and accept my patient, or my wife and children, or my friends. If I am a helpful person, then what I do or know or say can be helpful if my patient or parishioner can respond.

Russell Dicks wrote down his pastoral calls and prayers and also had his students write out their pastoral calls and prayers. This enabled them to study their relationships. Pushing the being mode one more step beyond Kuether leads to the quality and quantity of relationships.

Well before the fiftieth anniversary of the formation of ACPE, "the documents became the students themselves!" (Jernigan, H. January, 2000. Personal Communication). CPE became the study of relationships, both with the patients, their fellow students, the professional and the non-professional staff members and the Supervisor. In many centers, these seminars were called Interpersonal Relationship Seminars and in others they went by the name of group concerns seminars where relationships were frequently the focus of the group.

The study of the human document was no longer exclusively restricted to the patient. Dr. Boisen was unhappy with this development. His research interests in the spiritual meanings of life's difficulties, especially in psychoses, were no longer the exclusive interest in CPE. Dr. Boisen believed in the benefits patients received in discussing a case he presented to them in the group and also recognized that *the Christian Church with its class meetings and services and services of worship may thus be said to constitute down through the ages the outstanding exemplification of group therapy.* (Boisen, A. 1954. p. 37-38.)

This broadening of the supervisory focus did not, however, mean the end of the "ah-ha" or the transforming effect of CPE on so many of its students. CPE was often experienced as a "rebirth" experience giving new life to the student who felt freed from intellectual doctrines and religious legalisms.

This new discovery took place in the relationship with the supervisor(s) and fellow students as they reviewed case studies, studied verbatim records and reviewed "critical incidents." They critiqued one another in sermon seminars, clinical seminars and group concerns seminars. They examined their reactions to each other in the small group seminars. The accepting attitude of the supervisor helped create the freedom to explore the religious beliefs, practices and experiences of both patients and themselves. Thus, these relationships were examined and related to the students' own experiences and beliefs. In this way CPE was still concerned with living human documents.

In the last twenty-five years, one of the newer trends in ACPE has been the focus in some centers on "Theological/Spirituality Seminars" which was given a major emphasis as a result of the late Henri Nouwen's presentation at the joint conference in Detroit in 1976.

Bob Leas reported that *He mesmerized our ACPE Conference with insights and narrative about the rich journey of spirituality... The next year Art Bickel, David Middleton and I presented a workshop on "Spirituality in CPE." In the 1997 issue of the Journal of Supervision and Training in Ministry there were thirteen articles...* (Leas, R.   March 3, 2000.   Personal Communication.)

Herb Anderson, Art Bickel, George Fitchett, Susan Gullickson, Bob Leas, Janet Ryan, and Barbara Sheean are among many others who have made contributions to this new trend in supervision.

The venue of CPE has remained the same, wherever there are people in crisis and a certified supervisor in an ACPE accredited center.

A CHANGING WORLD

The majority of the CPE venues have remained the same: general and psychiatric hospitals, some parishes and other specialized institutions. Yet in the past thirty-three years they have all changed significantly. The reason for the changes: the United States and the world have experienced tremendous changes. Francis Fukuyama, a provocative thinker, observes:

> Over the past half century the United States and other economically advanced countries have made the shift into what has been called an information society, the information age, or the post-industrial era... This period, roughly the mid-1960's to the early 1990's, was also marked by seriously deteriorating social conditions in most of the industrialized world. Crime and social disorder began to rise, making inner-city areas of the wealthiest societies on earth almost uninhabitable... The decline of kinship as a social institution, which has been going on for more than 200 years, accelerated sharply in the second half of the twentieth century. Marriages and births declined and divorces soared; and one out of every

three children in the United States and more than half of all the children in Scandinavia were born out of wedlock. Finally, trust and confidence in institutions went into a forty-year decline. The perceived breakdown of social order is not a matter of nostalgia, poor memory, or ignorance about the hypocrisies of earlier ages. The decline is readily measurable in statistics on crime, fatherless children, broken trust, reduced opportunities for and outcomes from education and the like. (Atlantic Monthly. May, 1999. p. 55.)

But not only was the social situation changing dramatically, the religious life of the United States was also changing rapidly. Rear Admiral Richard G. Hutchinson, Jr. CHC, USN (Ret.) 1999, observes:

At its deepest level what happened in the sixties was a moral revolution. It reflected widespread rejection of the biblically based Judeo-Christian morality on which the nation had been founded and the emergence of a morality based on new, self-focused definitions of right and wrong. Its value system was essentially quite foreign to that of classical Christianity. The 'me-decades' of the sixties and seventies were to lead inexorably to the 'greedy decade' of the eighties. Self-centered values were in deep conflict with other-centered values. (p. 262.)

Chaplain Hutchinson also reports on the religious diversity:

The religious pluralism of American society poses challenges to the traditional character of the (military) chaplaincy. (p. 296.)

Both military and civilian chaplains, including the ACPE supervisors among them, are aware of the rapid changes in the religious identifications of hospital patients where many more list "none." Depending on the area of the country in which one lives, one may see more Muslims and Buddhists. At the same time, parish CPE programs have been located in Protestant or Roman Catholic parishes where the context is specifically Christian. Interest in CPE in the Jewish Community was awakened with Rabbis becoming certified and some Jewish seminaries strongly encouraging CPE.

Historian Arthur Schlesinger, Jr. (1999), summarized the situation as a result of all of these changes:

It (globalization and instant communication) plunges people into a vast anonymous arena beyond their comprehension and control. It thereby generates a backlash in the form of religious fundamentalism and ethnic tribalism. (p. 14.)

The past thirty-seven years of ACPE's history must be placed within the context of the changes and evolution within the centers where the programs are offered. Supervisors, seminaries and seminarians, and parish clergy were not working in a vacuum but were impacted by all of the changes around them.

The vast majority of ACPE supervisors and students have done their theological reflections within the context of Christianity and nearly all of the seminary members of ACPE are Christian, with only three Jewish member seminaries, one of which has two other widely separated locations.

Broader social issues were confronting America: the Cold War, the Civil Rights Movement, the War in Vietnam, the War on Poverty, Watergate, Irangate, and the sometimes severely changing economic conditions. Each and all of them also put pressures on most individuals and seminary students, ACPE centers, and religious denominations. Pope John XXIII and Vatican II, in their response to some of the same pressures, proved to be watershed events for the Roman Catholic institutions, parishes and parishioners. As a result of Vatican II, many Catholic priests and Sisters entered CPE programs to receive pastoral skills education, to reflect upon their call to the ministry and to engage in learning relationships with students from other faith traditions.

People everywhere are trying to comprehend and adjust to the current disruptions of contemporary life. In this period of very rapid transition, the ACPE, the centers and the institutions which house them, the seminaries and the churches are still seeking to meet the challenge of learning new ways.

In these many years, however, ACPE has been swimming upstream in the midst of still-powerful old currents and trying hard to stay upright in the waves which are washing over all institutions, political, economic and religious. The main denominations have until fairly recently furnished the vast majority of Supervisors. Due to the new waves of immigration, the settlement of refugees and other factors mentioned earlier, we are a much more diverse society, both ethnically and religiously, than almost at any time in the last half of this century. During this period of change more women entered CPE and military chaplains became interested in certification as supervisors. Students came from diverse religious traditions, interest in recruiting students from racial and ethnically diverse religious backgrounds increased, international pastoral care, counseling and education programs increased, and the issue of diverse sexual lifestyles started to be addressed in CPE.

ACPE's THREE MAIN FUNCTIONS: STANDARDS, CERTIFICATION AND ACCREDITATION

In contrast to earlier understandings, it is quite clear ACPE does not provide the CPE, it only sets standards, certifies individuals and accredits programs and centers. Centers provide the CPE!

STANDARDS
Dan DeArment is writing a history of the Standards in CPE and has contributed the following summary of his paper, to be printed later:

Since its founding in 1967, the ACPE has had approximately eighteen sets of standards. Notwithstanding pejorative or laudatory reflections... it can be agreed that there has been a lot of change going on. But in terms of the Bible and the history of various orthodox Christian groups utilizing the Bible as a source of authority, we can say we have no *canon.* Nor can the Standards be considered our Constitution –in terms of American history a legal or political venue.

What do we have in this written record? Simply put, we can say that the written record reflects what real people, living human documents, organized into a system describing what exactly was clinical pastoral education. This, the current Standards, they changed, and changed, and changed.

In reviewing these documents, I have been aware of the people who created this written record. I remember well the impact of these words of authority on my work as a certified supervisor (1968). I remember also, usually with fondness, the names of the many who wrestled and tugged with me over how to interpret these words. But the advantage of looking at the documents, quoting the documents, and making judgements about changes in the documents, is that the written record contains no footnotes, or by-line attributing any wisdom or folly to anyone. There is something of value in this kind of memory, and something of loss.

What is of value is that the written record reflects a system of ideas, not devoid of human touch, but as devoid of that touch as the written word can ever be. Part of what is lost, perhaps lost forever, are those connections between who said what and where, and what were the issues on both side of the debate that led to the final product. But there is potentially a greater loss. The literal words of the Standards usually led us to move ahead with creative CPE programs. But will the generations which follow be able to identify what CPE really is and was quite beyond the prosaic and sometimes dull words? As I collected the Standards from our 33 years of history, I was also writing poems about CPE. I understand better now just why I wrote: to place alongside the words of the system, some words of a more profound and mysterious process. (Poems included as an Appendix to his original paper) (DeArment, D. February 14, 2000. Personal Communication.)

The eight essential elements of cpe as listed in the 1977 Standards, and continued intact until 1996 are:

A specific time period (units of training) defined below:

> A unit of CPE is at least 400 hours of supervised learning
> A half unit is at least 240 hours of supervised learning
> A year of CPE consists of four consecutive units
> 1. The actual practice of ministry;
> 2. Detailed reporting and evaluation of that practice;
> 3. Pastoral Supervision;
> 4. An individual contract for learning;
> 5. A process conception of leaning;
> 6. A theological perspective on all elements of the program;
> 7. A small group of peers in a common learning experience.

Dan continues:

> In 1989 the current numbering system was added and the essential elements were listed as 122.1-122.9, with final item being added in the significant and hotly

contested "element" which stated *122.9. An evaluation of the student's CPE experience including final written evaluations by the student and the supervisor. The supervisor's evaluation will be available to the student within 30 days of the completion of the unit.*

Just as this writer sees the "essential elements" as a center point in the written record of developments in ACPE, I would likewise see the addition of the 9th item on written evaluations (first in 1987, and then in 1989) as a critical shift in the system –a small shift but one which reflected changes going on throughout the system. We were bigger, better organized, more accepted by the religious establishment and in other ways... successful. The Standards tell the story.

Changes in the Standards are considered at the request of the Certification Commission, and other various ACPE committees and the Office of Education. It is important for each center to be clear as to the standards under which they are applying. The Committee studies recommended changes and then the proposed new wording is sent out in the ACPE News for study and feedback to the Committee. If the overwhelming feedback on some proposals has been very negative, as has happened, the Committee has had to revise them, or even has withdrawn the proposed changes.

In order to simplify the three main tasks of ACPE, in 1993 the Board created a Task Force to report directions, procedures, and potential models relative to Certification, Accreditation and Standards. That Task Force reported to the Board in April, 1994, with many recommendations for each area: Accreditation, Certification and Standards. This was a watershed event and has made the entire process more "user friendly." (ACPE News. July-August, 1994. Vol. XXVII, No. 4. p. 1 ff.)

CERTIFICATION
Certification of supervisors had been one of the crucial tasks of the predecessor organizations. Originally the certifying body was called the accreditation committee and functioned as far back as the late 1940's. With fewer centers and supervisors the applicants met committees who were known to them by attendance at conferences and supervised by one or more of the Committee members. Malcolm Ballinger of the IPC had had one unit of CPE with Carroll Wise in 1935, had been an Army Chaplain in WW II, had assisted in one program and then was

informed in a letter by Rollin Fairbanks in 1947 that he was now a Supervisor! (Buford. 1990. Interview. p. 117.) Two CCT Supervisors, later ACPE Presidents, J. Lennart Cedarleaf and Charles Gerkin, after the evening social hour at a CCT Supervisors' conference at Lake Geneva, asked when they would meet the Committee. To their relief, they were informed that they had passed! (Cedarleaf, J. 1960. Personal Communication.; Gerkin, C. November 27, 1998. Personal Communication.)

The only written materials required included the Supervisor's reports to the seminary and a more extensive report to the CCT files, to be used if the student applied for further training. Questions were not confined to professional functioning but included many personal questions about family and spousal relationships! One key to who were certified was their ability to relate to the committee as a peer.

Because of the turf issues involved in merger, one of the best steps taken was to have the IPC and CCT accreditation committees observe each other in action, with the permission of the candidates. Each Committee decided that the other group's Committee was quite intelligent and the differences were not nearly as great as alleged. (Thornton. 1970. p. 178-179.)

This sharing also was taking place in most of the regions in 1966. By the time the CPE was formed in 1967, the task of "gate keeping," the act of certifying supervisors, was being resolved. The opportunity to serve on the Accreditation and Certification Committee (A&C) was coveted by many Supervisors who treasured these spots. These positions involved a lot of work and responsibility but also power in terms of the future of the organization. At one point, there was a deliberate choice to nominate and elect more active supervisors to balance some supervisors who were perceived as more passive and less likely to challenge applicants.

In 1974, the House of Delegates took the final action to split the one committee into two committees: Accreditation and Certification. Jasper Keith made an impassioned plea for both a separate committee and continuation of our recognition by the US Department of Education.

The steps to certification as an ACPE Supervisor have changed through the years. The late Ernest Bruder of St. Elizabeth's Hospital, Washington, D.C., saw the need for more extensive training for those desiring to become supervisors. He pioneered in developing a one-year residency program and then added a second and third residency program for supervision and other specialty programs.

Bill Russell, with long experience in the certification process, reported to the writer the following:

> The arrival of large numbers of women as well as other races and a more diverse student population began to change the face of CPE as well as challenge the way in which the supervision and education of CPE was carried out. This also challenged the way in which persons were educated in the art of supervision... In the certification process, there came to be more focus on students, group process, and the value of peer interaction as opposed to the dominate supervisor as the dominant personality. Also, there was a challenge to the elevated importance of intuition. Intuition without theory became problematic and, at times, harmful to students. Persons seeking certification needed to be able to give theory to what they practice... a challenge in the education of CPE supervisors. Part of this problem is that many of these persons are still being educated by persons who are unable to share with a student in supervisory education why they do what they do... This brings challenge from the Certification Commission when candidates arrive unaware that a new day has arrived on the CPE horizon. All of the above, on the whole, have been very positive movements in our organization. All of these changes have brought about ethical questions about where boundaries are in relation to supervisor/student. The changes in our society have appropriately challenged ACPE to pay attention to boundary issues in regard to student and supervisor and supervisor and persons in supervisory education. (Russell, W. March 3, 2000. Personal Communication.)

In the 1970's the steps were 1. Supervisor In Training (SIT), 2. Acting Supervisor, and then 3. Full Certification. The certification process included the applicant preparing written materials and an interview. In the 1980's the certification process was changed. The new steps became 1. Supervisory CPE (to learn supervision), 2. Supervisory Candidate, 3. Associate Supervisor, and then 4. Full Certification.

The new process required taking a test to examine knowledge; however, one had to take the test but not pass the test. Position papers were written to demonstrate theoretical and theological competence, and written reports of the supervisory process with students were provided to the presenter. The interview with the sub-committee determined how well one could integrate theory and practice and use the self in the supervisory process. Certification as an Associate and Full Supervisor are granted by the National Certification Commission. The test is no longer given. In the new process regions review applicants to determine if they are ready to enter the supervisory process. If so, they recommend Supervisory CPE standing. The next step is for the student to request regional approval to become a supervisory candidate which is the first step toward certification.

Over the years there have been many criticisms of the various interviewing groups because of the apparent unevenness of the Committee decisions. A number of candidates fail at the first meetings and most of them are encouraged to work on their issues and return after conducting additional units.

In earlier years, much more weight was given to the person's readiness to claim his or her authority as a supervisor. This was very important as the candidate affirmed one's self as a peer in meeting the authority of the sub-committee. On a rare occasion an unsuccessful candidate requested a re-hearing at the same meeting and the sub-committee reversed its decision upon meeting a more self-affirming candidate. Most often, however, sub-committees have helped those who were unsuccessful to identify areas of needed growth. After the needed work was done with one or more new groups of students, the candidates' appearances were usually successful.

Sub-committee decisions are sometimes easy to make and at other times are more difficult, especially when there is a split decision about the candidate's ability to function. Many supervisors have been certified on the basis of their potential rather than on present functioning. Earlier the sub-committees were more concerned with the person's ability to grow despite some current limitations. Some committee members were more generous and others more cautious about the individual's readiness. Some candidates come back a second or even a third time before being certified. Some unsuccessful candidates simply drop out of the process. There have always been concerns about the relatively high number of unsuccessful applicants at their initial appearances. A second question asked why it took so many years before the final "no" was given? It has been possible for a decision to be appealed, but most of the appeals are unsuccessful. For persons wishing to continue in the certification process regional committees have been very helpful to them.

Questions continually are heard about the reasons for the relatively low rate of approvals. The Commission reviewed a total of 489 applicants between 1989-1996 inclusive, and certified 298 of them, for an overall average rate of 60%. Individual year percentages varied from 52% in 1993 to 68% in 1994. (ACPE News. 1997. Vol. XXX, No. 2. p.10.)

Over the years the certification of supervisors has in many ways been considered the heart and soul of the organization. This is because the relationship between supervisor and students is considered vitally important in the CPE teaching/learning process.

Another change in certification through the years was the addition of a new appeals process. If the applicants received a negative decision of their certification request they could appeal the decision. An independent appeal panel would be constituted to review the commission's decision making sure it had followed its procedures and were in conformity with ACPE standards.

The increasing litigious nature of American society in academic circles has also effected ACPE supervisors and the Certification Commission.

Again, Bill Russell reports:

> From time to time attorneys have become involved concerning the failure to grant a satisfactory unit of CPE or a candidate being denied certification by the Certification Commission. This possibility has tended to reduce the spontaneity of interactions and trust levels of some involved in student/supervisory and supervisory/ supervisor relationships. This has been true of persons who have been grieved or had complaints filed against them by students. At times this reality has demanded more attention to the supervisory process and, therefore, has improved the very process itself.

ACCREDITATION: COMMITTEE AND COMMISSION

The function of the accreditation committee has been to apply the ACPE Standards to the institutions seeking membership as centers so that they can provide CPE according to nationally recognized standards. A bit of history is in order.

For many years, the CCT called its Certification Committee the Accreditation Committee. Initially the supervisor's certification was clearly understood to give the supervisor authority to establish a program in a center without further review. Well before 1967 it was finally clear to all CCT supervisors that accreditation applied to institutions and certification applied to persons. At the time of the merger the Accreditation Committee was given both responsibilities but certification was seen as its primary task.

After deciding that accreditation of programs and centers should be separated from certification, the Association applied to the US Department of Education for recognition as the national accrediting agency in the field of clinical pastoral education. This recognition was encouraged by the Association of Theological Schools (ATS) with the goal of strengthening the ACPE's standing as a national educational body in theological education. In 1969, the Executive Director, Charles Hall, received a letter from the US Commissioner of Education in response to the ACPE application, dated February 12, 1969, as follows:

> The Advisory Committee on Accreditation & Institutional Eligibility has recommended that the Association be placed on the Commissioner's list. The Association for Clinical Pastoral Education, Inc., is hereby added to the Commissioner's list of nationally recognized accrediting agencies/associations. (ACPE News. 1969. II, 3. p. 1.)

Succeeding renewals of this application have required the ACPE through its Accreditation Committee (and now as a Commission) to meet much more stringent requirements in the intervening years. This recognition moved the organization from independently deciding the accreditation process into dialogue with outside agencies such as the Department of Education and the Association of Theological Schools (ATS) regarding accreditation requirements and procedures.

This recognition, while not important to every center, assists ACPE with several governmental agencies, including the Veterans Affairs Department for educational benefits for veterans. Another benefit is that ACPE can sign student loan applications for the extension of payments so students can participate in CPE and pay their loans later. The US Immigration Service honors ACPE's requests for visas for foreign students to study at ACPE centers. It is also a solid recognition to other professional disciplines and institutions, including theological seminaries, about the educational standards of the Association. It probably didn't hurt to have this recognition when the Director of the Bureau of Health Insurance of HEW approved clinical pastoral education as a Medicare pass-through expense. The two offices are independent of each other. With proper documentation, CPE is seen as an allowable cost in Medicare on the same basis as those educational programs for nurses, dieticians and medical technicians. (ACPE News. 1973. Vol. VI, No. 9. p. 1.)

The primary goal of the Accreditation Commission is to foster the development of quality programs of Clinical Pastoral Education. To that end, they have sought to cultivate a consultative relationship with centers which invites dialogue and enables excellence in program development while supplying those standard documents necessary for the provision of a consistent program. The creative dimension of program design is freed up within the parameters set by the commission. Supervisors are able to focus on the provision of unique and quality programming for their students. (Nancy Dietsch contributed significantly to this section).

ACPE added public members to its Commission because of the increasing standards required in the light of public pressures. The process of accreditation is lengthy, with built-in safeguards and rights of appeal. It requires each center to have a professional advisory committee within the institution, including members from the community. This committee is responsible for the preparation of the submission of an institutional self-study, which demonstrates that the minimum standards are being met. Procedures with established time lines are set, which usually require a start one year before the date of the actual site visit. The site visit report is sent to the institution for review and comment. Then the total materials and the regional Accreditation Committee's recommendations are forwarded to the Commission for its decision.

The time required for these steps is taken away from the supervisor's pastoral care of his patients or clients and the supervision of students. These requirements, because they are written down are seen as being legalistic, as losing the 'heart" and "soul" of CPE. When added to the litigious nature of modern American society, and the student's right to appeal an unsatisfactory supervisor's report, something more personal has been lost from the earlier understanding and practices of ACPE.

Another frustrating element to some is the continuing evolution of the Standards. It is important for each center to be clear as to the date of standards under which they are applying.

In an effort to satisfy the standards, self-studies became exceedingly long, cumbersome, and redundant. Reviewers seemed punitive in their efforts to do their jobs adequately, and much of the spirit of the organization disappeared in its accreditation process. The Accreditation Commission began to revise its process, developing an accreditation manual, sample policies and procedures, questionnaires for program evaluation, and a requirement of a body of materials that would significantly diminish the amount of writing required at the time of the review. The Accreditation site team, regional committees, and the Commission sought to be more consultative in nature, thus enabling more dialogue through the process. For example, if the time line had changed in the standards and the change was missed by the center, the presenter (on the regional or national level) would call the center and ask for a correction, thus eliminating the necessity for a notation to be given. The number of notations being given droped considerably and the accreditation proocss has gradually been embraced as a helpful and consultative process. In the actual site visit process, a checklist has been developed which can give immediate impressions by the reviewers as to those items needing attention.

Several different terms have been used for centers seeking to initiate a program. Initially, it was Provisional Accreditation. Currently, it is Candidacy for Accredited Membership. The initial accreditation requires an annual report that addresses deficiencies identified in the site visit. The center proceeds to accredited Membership after it has provided several units of CPE and developed a track record. This should occur by the third year, with the possibility of a one year extension. (Dietsch, N. February 8, 2000. Personal Communication.)

In recent years, the Joint Commission on Accreditation of Hospitals (JCAHO) has recognized the influence of spiritual care in a patient's physical and emotional well-being. They have incorporated a review which is concerned with the spiritual needs of patients and how they are being met. This was one of the standards in the accreditation of psychiatric hospitals, partly through the efforts of leaders of the Association of Mental Health Clergy (AMHC). There was an effort to include that in the Joint Commission On Hospitals (JCOH) standards back in the late 1980's. At that meeting it was a tie vote and the chair cast the negative vote so they were not included. (Aist, C. 1980. Personal Communication.)

Now the JCAHO standards include the provision for the spiritual needs of patients. This past year the Congress On Ministry in Specialized Settings's (COMISS) accrediting program, the Joint Commission on Accreditation of Pastoral Services (JCAPS) has been granted advisory status with the JACOH, and a definition of "chaplain" is being developed. The focus is on spiritual care and outcomes rather than on the credentials of the providers of pastoral caregivers. The popularity of "spiritual" for nurses and others is leading many Pastoral Care departments to rename themselves as a Spiritual Care Service.

A number of supervisors have been concerned with outcomes of CPE in the past. CPE programs are now required by the Department of Education to identify and track outcomes of both patient care, professional development/employment, and supervision. Patient outcomes are tracked through spiritual assessment tools and the development of pastoral care plans. Alumni questionnaire and follow-up surveys are able to track the ongoing professional development and the employment of students in ministry fields.

PROFESSIONAL ETHICS COMMISSION (PEC)

This area of concern started out as the Judiciary Committee in 1967, but was renamed the Judiciary Commission in 1983 and authorized to render decisions which were final and binding in resolving conflicting interpretations of the Association's Constitution and By-laws and the ACPE Standards, Procedures and Guidelines, and interviewing complaints brought against an ACPE member, Supervisor or CPE program or against regional or national ACPE structure. (Constitution and By-laws. 1983. p. 19.) A few of their decisions were unpopular with some of the supervisors.

The Professional Ethics Commission shall make decisions regarding violation of ethics and professional practice. (Bylaws.

1997. p. 9.) Today, this Commission's function is to promote professional ethics in the ACPE proactively through education and responsively through case consultation. The guiding standards are in section 100 of the ACPE Standards, the Code of Professional Ethics. The main values are respect, competence, honesty and integrity, which influence the ACPE standards of practice and professional ethical conduct.

The Professional Ethics Commission Manual contains the complaint process. All centers are required to have a complaint process available and known to students/consumers. The fact-finding process, if it cannot be resolved locally, involves three PEC-trained panelists in each region to investigate the complaint. Neither party has the burden of proof –the Panel constructs the proofs from the evidence it assembles. The task of each party is to state clearly how the evidence relates to the truth of the allegations. The Panel's responsibility is to determine if a violation of ACPE Standards did or did not occur. All cases where violations are determined to have occurred are automatically referred to the full PEC for sanctions. The PEC will also consider cases on appeal. The decisions of the PEC are final and binding.

The PEC is composed of one representative from each region and the PEC chair. All members have full voice and vote, except in those situations where a case is being presented (the regional representative from that respective region does not vote). Legal counsel is regularly sought, though the attorney is not a member of the Commission.

The PEC sponsors workshops at annual conferences and is developing educational modules to be placed online for ACPE members to incorporate in developing professional ethics in their curricula. (Swaney, J., PE Chair. March 10, 2000. Personal Communication.)

CHANGES IN THE ACPE CENTERS

CPE Centers exist in radically changed institutions in the past thirty years by legislation, market forces, philosophical attitudes, and government policy changes, depending on which party is in control of the federal and various state governments. The US Supreme Court in a 1999-2000 series of 5-4 decisions have given more power to the several states with less power given to the federal government to solve national problems such as poverty, health care, etc.

Individual and states rights and responsibilities have come to the foreground in dealing with social problems. While there is a renewed importance placed on the role of volunteers and even in faith communities' efforts to help, national problems of poverty, homeless and health care are being left to the states and cities. Some states have set time limits on the length of time people can receive benefits. The efforts for a national health care system foundered on the lobby efforts of many, chief among them were those of insurance companies/physicians.

The health care field, especially hospitals, is now dominated by insurance companies, Medicare and Diagnostic Related Groups (DRG's). Now Medicare pays only for the admission diagnosis, not how many actual days it may take to care for the patient. The pressure is to reduce costs by reducing the length of hospital stays. The increasingly expensive drugs and nearly unbelievable new technologies have been difficult for not only patents and their families to absorb, but also for hospitals, physicians, and other hospital personnel, to say nothing of the HMO's, Medicare, Medicaid and insurance companies. Benefits have been reduced. The need to measure outcomes resulting from these changes has led to increasing pressure on physicians and all hospital employees. These changes may, in the long term, prove to be beneficial, but to implement them with fewer staff and less funding is problematical in the present. Providing CPE in this new environment is much more demanding, requiring more of supervisors in both orienting students and monitoring their pastoral care, most often with fewer hours in which to do it. The relatively unhurried atmosphere in which CPE originated has long since departed from most general hospital centers.

A 1999 informal non-randomized survey by this writer, with a 34% response rate from 125 long-time supervisors, asked about changes in settings which influenced CPE in comparison with earlier years. Only 14% reported no changes in the settings where they supervised CPE! Among the major factors, which made CPE more of a challenge (difficult), were: shorter patient stays (21%), while 16% experienced more difficulty due to downsizing and financial pressures. Increased staff expectations were an equal factor.

Both the new drugs and the pressures for de-institutionalization have radically changed psychiatric hospitals. Many state hospitals have been shifted to caring mainly for forensic patients. The basic in-patient psychiatric care is now being done in the general hospitals, but the HMO's and insurance providers provide strict limits on the amount of money and the number of in- and out-patients visits allowed. The President and the Alliance for the Mentally Ill, among others, are trying to get mental illness recognized on the same basis and with the same benefits as the physical illnesses, but progress is slow.

The Community Mental Health Act in the 1960's was to provide treatment in the community. But while patients were discharged into the community, the major funds to support the community mental health centers did not appear. If they did appear, they were insufficient to care for the many, many patients who were discharged from the psychiatric hospitals. The result has been many, many more troubled people, including veterans, as the homeless people, some with families are on our city streets in the daytime with evenings spent in homeless shelters.

We shall examine the results of these changes and our responses to meet them and the questions posed by Robert Powell in later chapters, but now take a look at 1975, our 50th Anniversary.

A REVIEW OF THE 50TH ANNIVERSARY CELEBRATION IN MINNEAPOLIS

1975 was a glorious year for ACPE celebrated the 50th Anniversary of the first unit of CPE in 1925 with Dr. Anton T. Boisen at the Worcester State Hospital, Worcester, Massachusetts.

The site of the Annual Conference and the Celebration was a new hotel, The Radisson South, Minneapolis, Minnesota. The Conference Program Committee, and the History Committee, with the Rev. J. Obert Kempson as Chair, had planned well. The Historical Dinner was titled "A Tough and Tender History." President-elect William Oglesby, Jr., chaired a panel consisting of representatives of the four predecessor organizations: Wayne Oates (Southern Baptist), Fritz Norstad (Lutheran), Carroll Wise (CCT), and Emil Hartl (IPC). Unfortunately, those videotapes are no longer available.

About 120 of the Founders and Nurturers of CPE were listed by region in the 50th Anniversary program, thirty-three of whom were deceased. (In 2000, over fifty-one have been added to the deceased list; only thirty-six of that group are still living.)

A group of distinguished speakers addressed the conference, including Robert Powell, Edward Thornton, Robert Preston, Peggy Way, Merton Strommen, Richard Children, James Nelson, Ross Snyder and Ross Snyder, Jr., and William Oglesby, Jr. These addresses are available in the 1975 ACPE Conference Proceedings. Powell challenged the audience with the several questions, which were listed on pages 13 and 14 of this history.

Dr. Oglesby challenged us, first, in our need to focus continuing attention to the theological dimensions of our faith, and also predicted:

> ...There will be a surge forward in relating and coordinating education for ministry in seminary and clinical settings... Two other areas seem to be of critical importance... The first has to do with a greater involvement of women in CPE at all levels... My guess is we are in the infant stage and have a great way to go. Finally, ...that CPE needs to break out of its middle-class shell. (p. 88.)

Regions had historical exhibits from the nine regions. One of the most unusual was an Orgone Box brought from the Jamestown State Hospital by Albin Sherve. Wilhelm Reich after his brilliant book, *Character Analysis*, moved into orgone therapy. This box was supposed to catch orgones. The FDA had ruled that this was an illegal device and Reich ended up in a Federal Prison. Some CCT supervisors had tried this theory and the CCT had been broadly labeled in a negative way because of that. Several tried the box in Minneapolis but experienced nothing. Al Sherve did not have to worry about federal prosecution because the box fell off his car roof and disintegrated en route back to Jamestown.

In 1975, the Directory showed the numbers in the various membership categories and they are compared with the same listings in the 1999-2000 Directory.

MEMBERSHIP FIGURES THEN AND NOW

The following information comes from the two ACPE Directories. It compares membership figures 1975 and 1999-2000.

	1975 Directory	1999-2000 Directory
Centers	329	358
Supervisors	465	534
Seminaries	117	117
Unattached	156	105
Retired	NA	173
Inactive	66	28
Vacant Center	NA	20
Supervisory Candid.	NA	115
Clinical Members	None	646

Compare the total units in 1975 and 1995, last year available by type:

	1975	1995
Basic	3538	4811
Advanced	1034	1481
Supervisory	227	441
Total:	4799	6733

In 1996 the total units were about the same: 6,894.

In 1996 the length of the units by type were as follows:

½ unit	83
½ extended	48
Extended	1513
1 Unit	5250
Total Units.	8894

CHANGES IN TYPES OF CENTERS AND CHANGES WITHIN CENTERS

The settings have changed. People are normally not hospital-ized for any length of time, even in psychiatric hospitals. Today's hospitals, in the main, have become intensive care hospitals, with sicker people. Many more patients are older persons, for we live longer today. Hi-tech diagnostic procedures and treatments, micro-surgery, quicker-acting and more power-ful drugs, with surgery being performed on people in their 70's and 80's, are all quite common. Open-heart surgery is common and more transplant surgeries are taking place with a higher success rate than in the past. There are fewer long-term in-patients in addiction programs and their stays due to insurance limits are short and some are even seen as outpatients. Orthopedic patients stay fewer days and are transferred to rehab centers or health care centers with rehab units for their physical therapy. CPE students have few long-term relationships with their patients in general hospitals, a real loss for students' learning as compared to earlier years.

There are far fewer CPE programs in correctional settings, even though there are many, many more people in correctional and penal settings. One of the fastest growing businesses in the US, outside of computers, is the building of prisons. There has been a 96% drop in correction-based CPE programs. We had twenty-five centers in youth, correctional and penal settings in 1975 and only one currently. However a few centers may provide placements in such institutions. At the same time, there were fifty-three psychiatric hospital centers in 1975 compared with only thirteen today, a reduction of 75%. Many of these hospitals house forensic patients with much longer stays. True, many general hospitals of any size have a psychiatric unit. But with shorter stays and more dependency on medications, they are not the same learning sites as were former mental hospitals.

Another regrettable development has been an alarming 94% decrease in ACPE centers in community mental health centers from sixteen to one, if the writer's review of all centers in the 1900-2000 Directory is reasonably accurate. As mentioned earlier, the Kennedy push for community-based treatment emptied many, many thousands from state hospitals without adequate follow-up care. Even today, persons with psychiatric diagnoses are tragically limited in the amount of money allowed for both in-patient and outpatient treatment.

Nine parishes were listed in the 1975 Directory and only one is listed in the current directory! The figure may be misleading. Satellite programs are usually related to general hospitals. Without a separate study of satellite centers, it may be possible that some satellite programs might be related to mental health centers. A number of general hospital programs have extended unit programs and even half-unit programs, which appeal to some parish clergy. Some may even bring their clinical material from their congregations. The parishes are also changing. The membership of the main-line churches is getting grayer. Evangelical and Pentecostal churches are growing rapidly while some of the main-line churches are hard put to maintain their current memberships.

The number of centers located in general hospitals has increased from 161 in 1975 to 298 in the current directory, an

83% increase. These figures include several hospitals where students are placed in satellite centers. One program, the Health Care Chaplaincy of New York City, places students in up to ten satellite centers, including a few non-hospital sites.

Every region had an increase in general hospital centers ranging from 38% in the Northeast to 145 % in the Mid-Atlantic. Pastoral counseling centers only have seven programs compared with twelve in 1975, a 42% decrease.

Centers in military installations have been reduced from eight to four, a 50% drop. Social service agencies as centers have been reduced from five to one, an 83% decrease. While included with the general hospital figures above, the VA Medical Centers have increased from three to sixteen – a 243% increase.

On the other hand, centers are now located in institutions which didn't even exist in 1975, i.e. Hospice Centers, of which there are now four. Urban training centers are not new, and ministry in inner cities is not new but CPE centers in such locations are relatively new. Palmer Temple, at St. Luke's Episcopal Church in Atlanta, pioneered one such a program by a different name. CPE programs in this venue are relatively new. There are at least three such programs today. (1999-2000 Directory)

Another large percentage increase has taken place with the CPE programs in retirement centers and rehab centers from two to ten, a 400% increase. One of the longest running programs for over 40 years was the one at the Goodwill Industries, Boston with the late Emil Hartl. Other centers are now located in spiritual renewal centers and in two seminaries themselves.

The Cluster concept, when two or more centers and one or more seminaries develop an integrated program, requires more vision, time and energy. This fell from seven clusters in 1975 to only two today, the Louisville and St. Louis Clusters.

The above figures show ACPE's increasing dependence upon general hospitals for the majority of its centers. Also, there are some good signs that centers are developing where there were no centers in the past. We have seen how changing social, economic and political forces impact not only the institutions but also the kind of services and clients for whom they seek to provide and also the services, which they no longer provide. Psychiatric hospitals and community mental health centers are examples. Without independent funding, the ACPE is quite dependent upon institutions that employ chaplains or clergy and who seek to provide training for community members and thus are willing to employ a certified ACPE supervisor.

There has been a vast increase in the number of residency training programs, which are available. Residency programs normally are for one full year, but some are only for the September to June time period. These programs are seen by both hospital administrators and supervisors as a means to provide pastoral care coverage. Even Introductory CPE programs, depending upon the maturity of the students, can provide an increased number of pastoral visits with inpatients and outpatients. A group of six students giving half time to patient visits provides at least twenty-four hours of pastoral care per week. If the supervisor spends half time with his students, that gives him a maximum of twenty hours per week with his patients. Those desiring certification need at least one additional residency year and a few centers have stipends for the supervisors in training beyond the single year residency.

Another important change has been the focus on outpatient care. Chaplains are being assigned to outpatient clinics. Home health care has been another focus where patients have much less mobility so the health care is brought to where they are, whether at home or apartment, etc. Some retirement centers are developing the concept of continuing care so that their residents can receive the health care in their apartments. Students in training centers in this type of program do not have to leave their building in order to make their pastoral calls. They can also be involved in longer term pastoral relationships.

The supervisors also put in incredible amounts of time, some professional but much of it personal, to keep alive the ACPE organization as it sought to adjust to changing expectations in a rapidly changing world. The national and regional Commissions, the Committees, the Councils and the governing of entities take an unusual amount of time and energy to keep alive the caring and inquiring spirit of ACPE. So the spirit of CPE has been living and breathing into the present and future and with its continued recognition as a national accrediting body by the US Department of Education. ACPE became more concerned with its standards and needed to meet, for some good reasons, the Department of Education's requirements for recognition as the National Accrediting Organization for CPE

THE NINE REGIONS

In 1975, ACPE's Executive Director was Charles E. Hall, who had assumed the post in 1968. ACPE was divided into nine active regions: Northeast, Eastern, Mid-Atlantic, Southeast, East Central, North Central, South Central, Southwest and Pacific. (See Appendix V for regional boundaries.) One of the results of the merger in 1967 was the elimination of the four national organizations and the creation of the ACPE with its nine regions.

The new regional boundaries corresponded, with some modifications, to the earlier boundaries of the CCT and IPC, two of its predecessor groups. Each region was organized in accordance with the Constitution, the By Laws, the standards, the accreditation and the certification processes of the ACPE. Each region had its own organization, so long as it conformed to the national constitution and by-laws. Each region elected four delegates to the House of Delegates, which was the national governing body.

Each region developed an identity of its own, partly depending on the number of supervisors who belonged to the previous four groups. The former IPC supervisors dominated the Northeast region, Baptists predominated in the Southeast, the Lutherans were more numerous in the North Central, and the CCT supervisors were strong in the Pacific. The other regions had fair numbers of members of each of the four predecessor organizations in their new regions.

Regions were originally encouraged to incorporate as non-profits (IRS 501-C-3). This gave them the benefit of freedom from state sales taxes in the state of incorporation, and a yearly audit was encouraged. Regions were free to develop their own financial patterns, some favored a more centralized arrangement and other regions were more "states rights" orientated and left more up to each center. Some regions charged the center a fixed fee per student where the amount depended on the number of student units conducted each year. For some, that fee was more substantial and made it possible for the region to pay the expenses of the supervisors to the regional meeting, and, in one region at least, for those of a representative from each seminary and for retired supervisors. Other regions charged much smaller fees. In those regions, the supervisors, seminary representatives, retired supervisors and retired members were on their own for expenses to the annual regional meeting. That regional meeting, separate from the national ACPE conference, was being held, since Dialogue '94, in the Spring with a smaller one held at the Annual ACPE Conference in the Fall.

The Board requested the regions to dissolve their corporations because they were a part of the ACPE, Inc. This has now been accomplished. Their financial statements are reported annually to the ACPE Treasurer and are included in ACPE's Annual Financial Report.

The regional Committees were originally the same as the ACPE national Committees. Executive Committees, Standards, at first, Accreditation and Certification, then later becoming separate Committees, Development, Finance, Research, History, Seminary Relations (in some regions) and later on, Public Issues, etc. Task Forces were quite common as both ACPE and its regions confronted new opportunities and problems.

Executive Committees were elected at the annual regional meetings and govern regions in between annual meetings. Regions were sometimes able to assist in developing programs in new CPE centers.

Each region has a regional Director, and at first they were joint employees of the ACPE, on the staff of the Executive Director, receiving an annual stipend from the ACPE. They also served the Regions. Their activities vary greatly depending upon the assignments given them by their respective Boards and the amount of time they have. Regions, which have had long-term regional directors, seem to do well. (See Appendix V for listing of Regional Directors.) Some regions have had much stability in having the same Director for twelve or more years, where as others have had to change every few years, depending upon the term of office, the director's enthusiasm or health or the region's endurance.

The regions gradually claimed full support of and direction for their regional directors and they worked for the region. Now the regional Directors meet annually with the Executive Director but in a mutually consultative fashion. Regional Directors normally carry their duties as an extra assignment from their center. Some spend as little as ten percent of their time on regional duties. Other regions have begun employing their Directors on a half-time basis. A few of the latter have been Supervisors who have recently retired.

Generally, regional Directors are selected upon application, recommended by the region's Personnel Committee and approved by the vote of the region.

Regional Directors (see Appendix V. for names), have had several duties, including being the central point for information for Supervisors, centers and seminaries. Each region publishes a newsletter on a regular basis (usually monthly) and the Director is normally the publisher, though one or more regions have assigned that responsibility to a paid editor/secretary. Directors encourage centers and Supervisors to be prompt in their reporting and in the fulfillment of regional and national responsibilities. They provide information to the Executive Committee and other Committees of the region. They staff the regional conferences and are often ad hoc members of Committees. They stay in touch with unattached/retired Supervisors. They often hear the first signs of difficulty that a Supervisor is having, and some of them have served as pastoral care givers to their flock of Supervisors, a pastor-to-pastor model.

Most regions had a difficult financial time supporting their fledging organizations. Each region received a start-up grant of $1,000.00 by the CCT as the CCT ended with a plus balance, which was also transferred to the ACPE treasury.

Over the years, the regions became financially stronger. In several key ACPE financial needs, individual regions contributed between $1,000.00 and $5,000.00 toward ACPE projects and fund drives. At the end of 1998, the combined nine regional assets total nearly $1,100, 000.00. (Independent Auditor's Report. April 19, 1999. Note 2.)

The main work of developing new training centers and reviewing them is done in the regions. Supervisors and regional directors are called in as consultants to local clergy groups, individual hospitals and other organizations who are interested in starting up ACPE programs. The writer personally made several initial visits as a regional director and knows of other regional directors who have played key roles in the initial start-up of chaplaincies and of ACPE programs.

Ever since the merger, some supervisors have felt that not only the national but also the regional organizations have been too large. The North Central Region, for example, after the merger had nearly as many centers and supervisors as did the entire CCT in 1967.

Geographically, small regions had an easier time to maintain a sense of fellowship and also had less expenses in getting together for regional and committee meetings. Some regions developed sub-regions and created a budget for them to facilitate both committee meetings and continuing education meetings. This was a practical necessity for regions with large geographical boundaries, e.g. Pacific. The North Central region and other large regions, for example, needed to choose Committee members on not only the skills and the interests of the Supervisors but also on their geographical location. Some regions created a continuing education fund based on the number of units in each state. These area balances enabled the Supervisors to plan at least one and sometimes two gatherings a year in addition to the regional and ACPE annual meetings. This provided good communication and fellowship as well as continuing education.

At the same time some supervisors did not feel that the regional gatherings were helpful in creating a sense of fellowship which had been developed in the previous organizations. Some regions developed sub-regional peer and continuing education groups to meet these needs. ACPE became more concerned with its standards and chose to meet the US Department of Education's requirements for recognition as the National Accrediting Organization for CPE. Some supervisors felt the size of ACPE and its emphasis to meet USOE's requirements as an Accrediting Association were so constricting that the original spirit of CPE had been lost. In 1987, Raymond Lawrence began to publish an Underground Newspaper. (See College of Pastoral Supervision and Psychotherapy (CPSP) section for more details).

Some regions developed recruiting programs where they visit a group of seminaries for a CPE day, inform students about CPE and their centers, and do admissions interviews for those already interested or required to take a unit of CPE. At least one denomination requires it ordination. Meetings with groups of faculty members may take place.

Because the ACPE Commissions and committees, with some exceptions, are made up of one or more representatives from each region, the Commission decisions are usually well received.

The system has been built so that the regional input plays an important part. Committee decisions made when ACPE had a

House of Delegates meant that the House had final approval of all decisions. As was mentioned earlier in the Governance Section, the change in 1992 meant that the Board of Representatives now has the final authority, except for nominating and electing officers and approving the budget. All recommendations go to the Board for prior approval.

Each region has a fascinating history of its own. Two regions have produced regional histories, The South East (Childs, B. 1987. *The South East Region of ACPE, A 20 year History and 20 Years in the Making;* and Summerlin, P. 1990. *A Chronological Survey of the Southeast region* ACPE 1978-1990) and the North Central (Thomas, J. 1996; Revised, 1997. *A Brief History of the North Central Region of the ACPE, Inc. 1967 –1987.*).

Fortunately, by the time of the 75th Anniversary, the *History of CPE in the Northeast, 1925-2000* (Homer Jernigan), The Eastern Region (Glen Asquith, Jr.) and the Pacific Region (Jerry Davis) have been completed. The East Central Region, Bob Leas, author, will be completed later this year.

The regions often initiated events such as joint regional meetings. The first such meeting between the North Central and Pacific regions was held in 1975 in Nevada. Joint, tri- and quad-regional meetings have been held occasionally since then. The Northeast and Eastern Regions have met together since 1996. Individual regions have co-sponsored or supported innovative CPE programs, and, on occasion, assisted in supporting area-wide conferences related to topics of interest to parish clergy and other professional groups. These initiatives came mainly from local ACPE centers.

The North Central Region of ACPE and the Central Region of the American Association of Pastoral Counselors joined together in 1978 in sponsoring a new Journal, The Journal of Supervision and Training in Ministry. It is still being published today, having just celebrated its 20th Anniversary. A report of that history, Rediscovering the Laws of Spiritual Life, the Last Twenty Years of Supervision and Training in Ministry, will appear in an issue in that journal. (Dr. Robert Fuller presented a summary at the NCR Regional Meeting, October 1999). Another region, the East Central, has been holding joint regional meetings with other cognate groups for a number of years. This meeting resembles meetings of the Canadian Association for Pastoral Care and Education.

Supervisors mainly, but not exclusively, from the North Central Region, challenged a decision of the ACPE Executive Committee to add an Associate Director to the staff on the floor of the 1996 House of Delegates. That led to the appointment of a Special Study Committee for 1977 and a new Special Study Committee began its task. That report was given in 1980. That will be covered in the Governance Section.

The regions are very significant players in the ACPE. Early on, significant differences were noted in the way regional certification Committees conducted their work and some regions tended to send candidates to the National Committee for Certification who were not ready to be certified. Early on, there were some pretty strong feelings about the way in which the Certification Committee dealt with its gate-keeping function for the ACPE. Then the Executive Committee could review its actions. Now the Commission's actions are not subject to review and appeals are now possible

GOVERNANCE

ACPE's original purpose included not only promoting CPE as a part of theological education and continuing education for ministry but establishing standards, accrediting CPE centers and certifying clergymen (sic) as supervisors of CPE. (ACPE Constitution and By-laws. 1967.)

Its members included all those accredited centers, certified Supervisors and the seminary members of the Association of Clinical Pastoral Educators, the Council for Clinical Training, Inc., the Institute of Pastoral Care, Inc., and the Department of Institutional Chaplaincy and Clinical Pastoral Education Lutheran Council in the U.S.A.

It was organized into seven further membership sections: Individual, Seminary, Institution, Agency and Parish, Cluster, Denominational, Council of Churches and Foreign.

House of Delegates: The affairs of this Association shall be managed by the House of Delegates, which shall have the power and responsibilities of carrying out the purposes according to the Constitution and By-laws. The House of Delegates shall consist of:
a. Four delegates from each region of this Association;
b. Two delegates selected by the American Association of Theological Schools;

    c. One delegate from the staff of the Department of
       Ministry of the National Council of Churches of Christ
       in the U.S.A.;
    d. Four denominational representatives chosen by the
       Department of Ministry of the National Council of
       Churches of Christ in the U.S.A.
    e. Five delegates at large elected by the House of
       Delegates. (ACPE Constitution & By-laws)

In 1973, the Executive Committee recommended several changes in the Constitution and By-laws. Regions were now to nominate one or two persons for each Committee but the House Nominating Committee will make a single nomination for each position to the House. Also, alternates are to be selected regions if the member cannot attend.

A constitutional amendment first vote was approved to create separate committees for Accreditation and Certification and to create the necessary By-law amendments for that change to take effect. A second 2/3's vote at the 1974 House meeting made that change official. In a similar manner, the number of Committee Chairs on the Executive Committee was reduced to exclude Finance, History, Judiciary and Research Committee Chairs.

The House of Delegates' Executive Committee's 1976 recommendation to employ an Associate Executive Director was soundly defeated. A following motion to create a one-year study committee to study the situation (regional/association finances) with one representative from each region was approved. As regional directors are no longer employees of the ACPE, their $1,000.00 annual retainer fees were to be returned to the regions, but another motion approved that total amount to fund the special study committee. Mark Anderson was chair of that committee and it brought in its report in 1977 as follows:

> This Committee shall conduct an in-depth study of the
> following Association concerns:
> A. Mission. On this 10th Anniversary of ACPE, this
> Committee shall review the history, purpose, goals and
> objectives of the Association, and anticipate the changing
> mission of the Association required for the 1980's;
> B. Structure. This Committee shall evaluate both
> Association and regional structures in the light of the new
> strategies required fulfilling the mission of the 1980's;
> C. Finance. This Committee shall evaluate funding

mechanisms of the Association in light of their appropriateness to the mission of the 1980's.

The Committee was charged with bringing annual reports to the House and a final report with recommendations to accomplish the mission for the 1980's and the means to do so. James Gebhart ably chaired this committee for three years and H. Rhea Gray served as the consultant. The president-elect served as one of the ex officio member of the Committee.

The House also accepted the recommendation of the Executive Committee to create a Personnel Committee and to develop a position description for the Executive Director. Each member studied and reported on at least one specific area and several good papers resulted. As proposals were discussed and developed, the members kept in touch with their regions and extensive feedback was received.

The composition of the Executive Committee had been changed from five members elected by the House to include the chairs of all seven of the standing Committees plus two at-large members elected by the House.

The final recommendations, most of which were adopted by the 1980 House of Delegates and some deferred until the 1981 House, were far reaching. A few did not pass. One, by the late William J. Johnson, Jr., envisioned an Academy of Pastoral Care Organizations, toward which several organizations have been working on and off since then. Other efforts included Dialogues '88 and '94. The current Five Presidents' Initiative begun by then President William Baugh is still meeting together. Every area of ACPE activity was studied carefully. Partly as a response to the 1970's challenges for a wider participation in government, the House of Delegates created a General Assembly in its place. (Special Study Report. 1980.)

Specific recommendations were adopted in 1980 and 1981. The Annual Conference Committee was continued and new Committees of the Board included: new Emergency Credentials Committee, an Endowment Grant Committee, A Foundation Committee, and a History Committee. Advisory Councils for Seminaries and Denominational/Faith Group Councils were created. A new category of membership, Clinical Member, was widely debated in both the Committee and the House and was finally adopted. One of the ideas supporting it was that we ought to have a way to receive feedback from the users of CPE, those who have had at least four units of CPE, two basic and two advanced. The other reason was that they should be welcome in our governance and meetings. The budgetary aspect was also of some significance.

By 1988, however, Duane Parker reported both a fuzzy line of authority in ACPE and a financial crisis. The Board voted to give Governance and Finances the top priorities for the next two years. The 1990 General Assembly appointed a special GA Governance Group with the late William Nisi as the chair. A preliminary report, including a Governance Manual was adopted in 1991. A Governance Manual, previously adopted on July 1991, was revised in July 1992, and subsequently adopted in May of 1995 and 1997. The manual is subordinate to the By-laws but spells out interpretations of the By-laws and procedures to implement the ACPE governance. Nine options for changes in governance, which included wider participation, clarify lines of accountability, provide better legal protection for the organization and its elected representatives, and finally, to have a smaller representative group serve as the "Board of Directors." It is interesting to note that this latter change was following the pattern of corporate America. The time for lengthy discussions and waiting until a consensus was arrived at in a larger body was over.

On November 20, 1991, the General Assembly approved, after heated objections by some, the By-laws prepared by John C. Joyner of Weeks and Candler, P.C., Decatur, GA. A smaller body, about twenty-five, was to be given much more power. The major recommendations were adopted the next year and became a part of the By-laws by 1992: a revision of the Constitution and By-laws to eliminate the Constitution; to create new By-laws and a governance manual, to create a Board of Directors in whom the legal responsibility will rest. The Board now appoints the Committees and Commissions upon recommendation of the regions. The General Assembly no longer exists. An Annual Meeting elects a Treasurer and a Secretary in alternate years. It conducts a nominating convention every other year to elect two candidates for the office of the President-elect, who will be elected by mail ballot. The Annual Meeting continues to approve changes to the By-laws, hears Board reports and adopts the budget.

The By-laws established three commissions: Accreditation, Certification, and Professional Ethics. The Board established three committees: Standards, Nominating and Professional Ethics. It has the power to establish other Committees. Members of the Commissions and Committees shall be appointed by the Board upon nomination by the regions. (ACPE By-laws. 1992, 1998.)

There was initial strong opposition to some of these recommendations but the basic one was that the By-laws Committee had become another special study committee and had exceeded its mandate. This also eliminated several committees, including Development, History, Public Issues and Research. At the same time, the idea of Networks was developing as a way to harness the interests of members and to provide linkages across the ACPE without incurring any financial responsibility, one concern.

Two new categories of membership have been added: Supervisory Candidates with voting rights, & Retired Supervisor Membership. In May 1996, Clinical Members were defined as having completed four units or more units of CPE as recognized by the ACPE in 1996. Two new categories of group membership were added: first, Network member for special interest groups approved by the Board, and second, International Affiliate Organization for Organizations/Entities in Other Countries Designated for Membership by the Board

WOMEN IN CPE AND ACPE

We are now ready to deal with one of Dr. Oglesby's challenges in 1975:

> Two other areas seem to be of critical importance. The first has to do with a greater involvement of women in CPE at all levels... My guess is we are in the infant stage and have a great ways to go. (ACPE Conference Proceedings. 1975. p. 88.)

Helen Flanders Dunbar, at Anton Boisen's suggestion, had worked one month in the summer of 1925 in the Social Service Department at Worcester State Hospital and thus they began an important relationship, though she was never technically a CPE student of his. There were a number of women, including at least one occupational therapist (known to the writer) in Mr. Boisen's early programs. Relatively few women had been enrolled in the early CPE supervisory programs in New England because few of the major denominations got around to ordaining women until much later (Methodists and Presbyterians, 1956). The early women who enrolled came out of the religious or Christian education programs, such as Louise Long from Garrett who came to Elgin in 1945. Women chaplains had an impact on later male supervisors. Both Charles Hall and Max Maguire report being influenced to take CPE by Kathryn Millsap, a clinically trained chaplain in one of Dr. Boisen's group in 1937. Mary "Louise" Long was certified by the CCT in 1949. The second woman, Helen Tytus Terkelsen, was certified by the IPC in 1960 at the age of 51. (Buford, P. Th.D thesis. 1997. p. 6, 152-182, 231-245.)

Paula Buford reports for the 1962-1867 period only that only 7% of the total number of students were women. (1997, p. 387.) Only two women, Helen Terkelsen and Florence Lewis, both IPC Supervisors, entered the ACPE as full Supervisors.

The 1975 Directory only lists ten women as active Supervisors and five as unattached. The active women were concentrated in the New England area (3), in the Eastern (3) and in the North Central Region (2).

The current directory lists at least 142 active women out of 670, the total number of supervisors, or 23%. Yet, it is an increase of 1320% over the ten in 1975. The eighteen unattached women Supervisors represent a 260% increase over the five in 1975. Five women are listed as inactive and eight have retired in 2000.

The more important figure is the number of fifty-five women among the 155 Supervisory Candidates, 35% now as contrasted with the current percentage of 23% of active women Supervisors. The movement is in the direction of more women Supervisors. Yes, the challenge from Dr. Oglesby in 1975 is being met.

Women have been more active in leadership circles. Helen Terkelsen joined the Executive Committee in 1972, was elected its Secretary that same year and was elected as Vice Chair for 1980-81. Sister Monica Lucas was the first Roman Catholic to be elected Secretary in that general time period. A Study Group of Six Women Supervisors in CPE consulted with the Executive Committee. The House of Delegates asked the President to appoint an Ad Hoc Committee to develop further colleagueship with women. (ACPE News. 1979. Vol. XII, p. 2, 11 ff.) Under Sister Monica Lucas' leadership, the group adopted a Mission Statement:

...We are committed to a common ministry. That ministry is impaired because of the pain and injustice of broken collegiality between women and men. We commit ourselves and challenge our colleagues to join in a prophetic witness with hope toward reconciliation. (ACPE News. October, 1979. No. XIV. p.11.)

A Task Force on Women's Issues decided to focus on collegiality between women and men instead of focusing only on women's issues. Kathy Turner and Dick Sellers created a collegiality game for CPE centers to use in focusing on gender issues.

Among the first women supervisors to be certified after 1967 were the following: Shirley Causey, Shirley Herman, Sister Pat Johnson (first Roman Catholic) Maxine Walasky, Sister Michelle Harmon, Emily Jean Gilbert, Sister Monica Lucas, Ruth Ellen Wagner, Marlyne Goven Cain, Janet Ryan. Mary Wilkins, Kathy Turner, Sister Dorothy Cotterell and Peggy Ollman Kieras.

Joan Hemenway became the first woman Regional Director for the Eastern Region in 1983, but it took until 1990 for the second one, Jo Clare Wilson, in the East Central Region, to be selected. Deborah Whisnand, selected in 1996, continues as the Regional Director for the Southwest Region.

ACPE took twenty-five years to elect its first woman President, Kathy Turner, but it only took six more years before it elected Jo Clare Wilson as its second woman President. Sherron Hughes-Tremper was the unsuccessful 1999 candidate for the office of President Elect.

Women Supervisors have profoundly influenced the educational process in ACPE as well as taking an increasing place in its organizational life. Women's cultural perspectives about suffering, pastoral care and ministry have been more on the "heart" side.

The cultural role expectations for women in our culture have been in the direction of being more intuitive, sensitive and relational. Their presence has changed the perspectives of both Supervisors and students in training.

They have helped the organization become more aware of the sexual dynamic inherent in the supervisor-student relationships, including the misuse of power by male supervisors on some occasions. As a result the ACPE adopted a much stronger and clearer code of professional ethics.

The increasing number of women supervisors was difficult for some male supervisors to handle. Many were insensitive to patterns of speech and behavior which had been acceptable before the era of women's liberation. No one will ever know about the capable women who dropped out of the CPE process for that reason. No one will ever know how much courage it took for some women in a lesser power position to challenge male supervisors and remain in the supervisory process. The women had to request that at least one woman serve on each Certification Committee!

Paula Buford makes some thoughtful observations about the early women in pastoral care and what it was like to be the only woman in a group of five male students. Thelma Dixon Murphy reports:

> I didn't feel that I was accepted as one of them. I was something different... Seems to me that the men I associate with (then and in later training) didn't know what to do with a woman. They felt that they should be doing or not doing something. You could not just be an individual like other individuals... Some of their hostility to women was directed to me somewhat. (p. 122-124.)

A male supervisor put it this way:

> It was o.k. ...for a group of good-ole-boy Southerners to use profanity and sexual words. The moment a woman came in, it was like bringing in your mother with you. And that immediately created a restraint, which that woman got credit for (because the woman trainee) symbolized virtue, honor and restraint. (p. 125.)

Paula Buford reports:

> The fear and mystique that comes with placing women "on a pedestal" is illustrated in Anton Boisen's relationship with the significant women in his life. According to Carroll Wise, three women (his mother, Alice; his unrequited love; and a female training student) contributed to Boisen's (later) psychotic break of 1930. (p. 125.)

Sister Pat Johnson remembers:

> Being valued as a nurturing mother within her training
> groups. She believes that women were welcomed into
> training groups in the late 1960's because of the
> emphasis on helping the men to "get in touch with their
> own feelings" and because of the Jungian emphasis on
> persons' balancing the masculine/feminine polarities in
> their personalities within the Institute of Pastoral Care.
> Women were feeling experts, thus functioning as
> "emotional prostitutes" for the men with little regard for
> their own emotional and professional development.
> (p. 126.)

Mary Wilkins of the North Central Region reports her efforts to
get the women together in her hotel room at the 1973 Annual
Conference in St. Louis. Mary worked with a group of women
seminarians in Chicago and planned three events:

> (1) A Women and CPE conference in Chicago in the Fall
> of 1973 for Chicago area women in CPE (although three
> women in Atlanta heard about it and made the trip to
> Chicago for this event);
> (2) a Continuing Education Event for Supervisors in the
> Northern Illinois sub-Region on Women's issue in CPE;
> (3) a Workshop on Women's Issues for Supervisors at
> the Annual Conference in 1974. (Wilkins, M. February
> 10, 2000. Personal Communication.)

Mary also conducted an early all-women's group but observed in
another context the following:

> The need for a change in educational emphases for
> women students from a focus on feelings and
> relationships which had been traditionally identified as
> areas where women had "natural" gifts toward an
> emphasis on reflection on the practice of ministry and
> theological reflection, where women had traditionally
> been excluded and thus needed to find their own voice.

Women in all the cognate groups held a special pre-Dialogue
'88 event, which was a rallying point for women in the several
organizations. Women instituted an annual breakfast at the
annual conferences and now the men have instituted a men's
breakfast! Not to be overlooked are the new contributions of
Roman Catholic sisters in CPE programs at the end of the

1960's and early 70's. With Vatican II many sisters changed their vocations from teaching to pastoral care and contributed greatly as students and as supervisors.

JEWISH INVOLVEMENT IN CPE

According to the CCT Annual Catalogue, 1952-53 CCT, Rabbi I. Fred Hollander was certified in 1949. (Rabbinate. 1946. Yeshiva University.)

After that date he supervised for several years at Bellevue Hospital and the Federal Detention Headquarters, New York City. He received a Certificate in Applied Psychiatry for the Ministry in 1951 from the William A. White Institute of Psychiatry, New York, and was Associate Director 1949 to date (1953) of the Institute for Pastoral Psychiatry, New York Board of Rabbis. Rabbi Hollander later moved to Israel.

Rabbi Jeffrey Silberman, certified in 1988, was the earliest Jewish supervisor in the ACPE and served a term as Eastern Regional Director! Chaplain Phyllis Brooks Toback has been supervising at Christ Hospital, Oak Lawn, IL, since 1989 and has been quite active in the North Central Region. Other rabbis currently supervising aare Israel Kastenbaum, Julie Schwartz, Myhal Springer and Bonita Taylor. (See Seminaries section for information about Jewish Seminaries.) (Tobak, P. March 21, 2000. Personal Communication.)

ROMAN CATHOLICS & CLINICAL PASTORAL EDUCATION

The first Roman Catholic priest to be certified as supervisor was John D. Allemang, a diocesan priest from Milwaukee, who ran the program at the Wisconsin School for Boys, Wales, Wisconsin. The Council for Clinical Training certified him in the Fall of 1967, just before the merger into ACPE. The second priest was Francis Garvey, a diocesan priest from Kandyohi, Minnesota, whose training and supervisory background was the Institute for Pastoral Care. The first priest who came through the ACPE Certification process was Donald Shmauz, Allemang's successor at the Wisconsin School for Boys.

A number of Roman Catholic sisters received Acting Supervisory status as early as 1973, but the first one to be fully certified was Patricia Johnson in 1975. Sisters Michelle Harmon and Monica Lucas followed in 1976. They and their many successors have contributed to ACPE.

In 1965, the National Association of Catholic Chaplains was organized. In 1966, the Administrative Board of the bishops, meeting in Washington, voted $8,000.00 per year for three years to fund the new association. By 1967, the United States Catholic Conference Board of Examiners was accrediting programs and certifying chaplains. By 1970, the ACPE training was even being offered in some Catholic institutions. Many Catholic priests and sisters sought training and certification in ACPE. The Board of Examiners was abolished in 1983 in favor of the new USCC Commission on Certification and Accreditation. (The NACC: A Twenty-Year History 1965-1985. Special Publications of the National Association of Catholic Chaplains. August, 1985. Vol. 1, No. 2.) Many Catholic ACPE supervisors have been dually certified, beginning with Francis Garvey who conducted CPE at the Willmar State Hospital, Willmar, Minnesota. The presence of Roman Catholics, both priests and sisters, as Supervisors in ACPE has increased the diversity of the programs and enriched the ACPE life. The relationships between the two organizations have had their ups and downs during the years, especially in the area of reciprocal recognition of each other's certification of supervisors. The Collaborative Steering Committee is working on areas of mutual cooperation. (see Section on Interorganizational Cooperation.)

RACIAL, ETHNIC MINORITIES, LATER CHANGED TO MULTICULTURAL

The first African-American (black was the term used then) to be certified by the CCT was Merrel Booker in 1948. He supervised programs at Freedman's Hospital in Washington, D.C. for several years before returning to education. When the IPC merged into the ACPE four supervisors of color, Henry Brooks, Jack Clark, Oscar Phillips and Guy Outlaw were the only active supervisors of color, and they were members of the American Baptist Convention. In 1972 Merrel Booker re-entered as an Acting Supervisor in the North Central Region at a Garrett Theological Seminary (Evanston) Community Hospital (Evanston), Provident Hospital (Chicago) Joint program through his retirement in 1976. Henry Brooks, Oscar Philips and Guy Outlaw continued supervising into the 1990's.

Dr. Oglesby challenged ACPE to break out of its middle class status. He could have added "to break out of its WASP cultural status." CPE had been a white, Anglo-Saxon Protestant program which did include women and minority students as students. But it took a long time before many minorities including Afro-Americans became supervisors.

The Special Study Committee Report stated:

> The ACPE Consultation on Blacks in CPE is preparing to provide information about CPE to the Black Churches. The consultation wrote, "The Black Church needs CPE and CPE needs the Black Church.'" (1980. p. 16.)

Many efforts have been made to reach out and some supervisors have supported programs to reach out to minority pastors. The challenge is still present!

The percentage of REM supervisors is very low compared with numbers in the population and the total number of REM churches. Two of the newer generations of African American supervisors are Retired Supervisor George Polk and Cameron Byrd, who until 1996 was Chair of the REM Network.

The first African-American woman certified as a full supervisor was Thanda F. Ngcobo (4/20/85) followed by Cecilia Williams (10/29/80), Teresa Snorton and Delois Brown-Daniels (11/2/90) and Gail Kennebrew Poindexter (4/30/94).

The Racial Ethnic Minority group was first formed as a Task Force in 1981 with George Polk providing the leadership. It organized in 1988 to hold its first annual conference at Howard Divinity School, Washington, District of Columbia with about sixty attendees. A number of non-REM supervisors have participated on a regular basis. J. Edwin Lewis and Cameron Byrd succeeded George Polk as Task Force Chairpersons. Another early supervisor was Eugene Robinson. This REM meeting provided a way to involve and recruit seminary students for ACPE and to encourage the efforts to get more REM members in supervisory training. More and more participants have attended these lively meetings each year. These are occasions for CPE students to be more involved with the REM supervisors. A number of non-REM supervisors have also participated on a regular basis. At the 10th Anniversary of the REM Invitational the following founders were recognized:

Rev. George Polk, Rev. Richard Stewart, Rev. Dr. Claudette-Copeland, The Dr. Carolyn McCrary, Rev. Cannon Dalton Downs, Rev.Urias Beverly, Rev. J. Edward Lewis, Sr., Rev. Thanda Ngcobo, Rev. Cameron Byrd and the Rev. Henry Brooks. (ACPE News. 1997. Vol. XXX, No. 3, I.)

REM, like 11 other groups in ACPE has become a Network. The REM Invitational programs have included outstanding speakers from seminaries and other professions as well as REM members. The time for fellowship and sharing are important parts of the meeting.

Over 300 participants were present at their 13th meeting in Raleigh, North Carolina this February. While the majority are African-Americans, other racial, ethnic and religious minorities or other interested ACPE members are welcome at the February REM Invitational Conferences and at the REM Network meetings at the Annual ACPE Conference.

George Polk was the unsuccessful candidate for President-elect in 1982 when James Gebhart, Chair of the Special Study Committee, was elected. In 1990, Kathy Turner, the first woman to run for the office, defeated Urias Beverly. In 1992, the nominating convention selected Urias as the only nominee and he was elected and served as President from 1994-1995. REM women took active parts in regional affairs. Delois Brown-Daniels was elected chair of the North Central Region in 1996. Cameron Byrd, now Chair of the 2000 Annual ACPE Conference in Arlington, Virginia, turned over the mantle of REM leadership to Teresa Snorton in 1996. Teresa resigned in late 1999 to become the new Executive Director of ACPE. Teresa has two distinctions: the first woman Executive Director of ACPE and the first member of REM to be selected for that leadership responsibility. Patricia Wilson Robinson was elected Chair of REM for 2000-2003. (Snorton, T. February 22, 2000. Personal Communication.)

Henry Brooks, Supervisor and Professor at Andover Newton Theological School estimates that 8-12% of the clinical pastoral trainees at that school between the 1950's and 1970's were African-American because this training was required of all S.T.B. students. (Buford, P. p. 402.)

THE OFFICE MOVES FROM NEW YORK TO DECATUR, GA.

Between 1967 and 1984 the ACPE office was located at the Inter-Church Center, 475 Riverside Drive, New York. As early as April 1980, Executive Director Hall had suggested the removal or relocation of the office from New York City. (ACPE News. April, 1980. 6.) He reported that some regions were considering putting in a bid for the office. Hall's personal preference was outside of New York City in a lower cost area. Hall also announced that he planned to retire to the Midwest within a few years. The 1980 Special Study Committee recommended the creation of a site committee to establish criteria and make a recommendation. That committee, evaluating the five cities, rated them fairly close, with Chicago receiving the slightly highest score.

In the meantime, a well-organized effort on behalf of the Southeast Region, led by Jasper Keith, came to the House of Delegates with a strong recommendation to move the office to the Atlanta area, including some strong inducements by the Presidents Chief Executive Officers of Emory University, Columbia Theological Seminary and the International Theological Center. Some special funds were already available for the move to Atlanta. By a two-thirds majority, the House chose Atlanta, and the date was to coincide with Director Hall's retirement in 1984. (ACPE News. November-December, 1982. Vol. XVI, No. 9-10. p. 5.)

This same issue of the ACPE News carried the announcement that applications for the position of Executive Director were being welcomed and a prospectus was enclosed. The Executive Committee and the Chair of the Personnel Committee, Max Maguire, actively sought applications from women and minorities. In October 1993, the name of Duane Parker was presented to the General Assembly and he was approved by it as the new Executive Director to begin July 1st, one month prior to Director Hall' resignation. Consultation duties with Charles Hall began prior to his move to the Atlanta area. The General Assembly also voted to purchase two units of a condominium office building at 1549 Clairmont Drive, Decatur. Over $71,000, including pledges totaling $37,00.00 from regions, was raised toward the $202,500.00 purchase price. An additional $80,000.00 will be needed to equip the office and provide for the overlap of directors.(ACPE News. September-October, 1983. p. 3.)

2. Group Photo of History Network Whose Idea it was to Publish This Text.
Rear: O. Chappell Wilson, Jr.; Robert Leas; Jerry Davis. Front: Myron
Ebersole; John Thomas; Ray Bailey. *Acknowledgements, p. 6.*

3. Homer Jernigan.
Acknowledgements, p. 6.

4. Edward Thornton. *Brief History,*
p. 11

5. Charles Hall. ***Brief History, p. 11.***   6. Joan Hemenway *P. 11.*

7. Seward Hiltner, Seated. ***Early***   8. Carroll Wise. *Early Pioneers.*
Pioneers, p. 15

9. Wayne Oates, Edward Thornton, and Aldine Anderson (1983).

10. John Billinsky. *Early Pioneers.*   11. Frederick Keuther. *P. 15.*

12. Malcolm & Marjorie Ballinger.   13. J. Obert Kempson. *50th*
Certification, p. 22.   *Anniversary, p. 33.*

14. History Panel at Chicago. From Left: J. Lennart Cedarleaf, Wayne Oates,
John Thomas, and Emil Hartl (1984).

15. Special Study Committee. From Left: Robert Morris, William Johnson, Ray Otto, James Gebhart, James Gibbons, John Thomas, Robert Eades. *Governance, p. 45.*

16. Louise Long, First Woman Supervisor. *Women in CPE, p. 49.*

17. Installation of Kathy Turner. From Left: James Gebhart, Kathy Turner, Julian Byrd, Max Maguire, Jasper Keith, Aldine Anderson, and John Thomas. *Women in CPE, p. 50.*

18. Installation of Jo Clare Wilson (Right. Kathy Turner, Left). *Women in CPE, p. 50.*

19. Donald Shmauz, First ACPE Roman Catholic Supervisor. *Roman Catholics in CPE, p. 53.*

20. George Polk. *Racial, Ethnic Minorities, p. 55.*

21. Cameron Byrd. *Racial, Ethnic Minorities, p. 55.*

22. Thanda Ngcobo, San Diego 1985. *Racial, Ethnic Minorities, p. 55.*

23. Henry Brooks. *Racial, Ethnic Minorities, p. 56.*

24. John I. Smith and Charles E. Hall, at Dedication of Plaque at Worcester State Hospital. *Executive Directors, p. 70.*

25. Aldine Anderson and Duane Parker (1982 Campaign). *Executive Directors, p. 70.*

26. Helen Patton. *Executive Directors, p. 72.*

27. Russell H. Davis (Left); Urias Beverly (Right). *Executive Directors, p. 72.*

28. Stuart Plummer. *Executive Directors, p. 73.*

29. Teresa Snorton. *Executive Directors, p. 73.*

30. Past Presidents. From Left: Charles Gerkin, J. Lennart Cedarleaf, John Thomas, Aldine Anderson, Al;bert Meiberg, James Gebhart, William Lgelsby and Jasper Keith. *Presidents, p. 73*

31. Henry Cassler. *Presidents, p. 73.*

32. W. Clement Stone, First ACPE Appreciation Award. *Finances, p. 75.*

33. Past Presidents. Rear: Urias Beverly, Jo Clare Wilson, William Baugh, Duane Parker (Past Executive Director). Front: John Thomas, Max Maguire, Kathy Turner. *Presidents, p. 73.*

34. James Gibbons. *Research, p. 84.*

35. 1987 Conference held in Melbourne, Australia. *International Cooperative Efforts, p. 89.*

36. Public Issues Committee. From Left: Joan Hemenway, James Gebhart, Myron Eberson, Robert Carlson, and Arthur Schmidt. *Networks-Public Issues, p. 98.*

37. Bust of Dr. Anton T. Boisen, by William J. Johnson, Jr.

Duane Parker knew the Executive Vice President of the Kresge Foundation from Rhode Island days. The next year Charles Hall, President elect Jap Keith and Duane Parker prepared a challenge grant to the Kresge Foundation and its Board approved a grant of $75,000.00 on condition that ACPE raise $108,605.00 in five year pledges to receive it and complete the building transition project. (ACPE News. September-October, 1984. Vol. XVII, No. 8. p. 8.)

Regions were encouraged to claim ownership of the new office through financially contributing to the purchase and preparing gifts to be hung on the office walls. The gifts represented the uniqueness of each region.

EXECUTIVE DIRECTORS

John Smith, then Executive Secretary for IPC, began in January, 1967, serving as Joint Executive Director. He published a monthly Newsletter until September 1968. John was elected as the first ACPE president in the Fall of 1967 but he continued to serve as interim Director. He made trips to the regional meetings during the first crucial year of the merger and got ACPE off to a running start. His irenic spirit and presence served ACPE well in this beginning year. He turned over the interim Executive Director's position on September 1, 1968 to the new Director Charles E. Hall, Jr.

Charles Hall served from 1968 through 1984. James Gebhart, a past President describes well the excellent leadership Charles Hall provided throughout those sixteen years. (Gebhart, J. January, 2000. Unpublished Presidential Reflections. p. 5.)

> Chuck Hall and Duane Parker: extraordinary persons cast into critical transition who served ACPE with prodigious and inspired leadership... These two men were truly called to lead us around corners of history... Chuck Hall was the quiet, unassuming, persevering and often lonely captain.
>
> His mandate: to serve as the Executive Director of a central office while never limiting the powers of traditional regional leaders. The personalities who had formed the IPC and the CCT had no intention for any diminished influence in the newly formed Association... He had no power base, no coalition of support. He too often

suffered indignities alone, but to his credit he never discredited his opponents or resorted to any petty in-fighting. He was a man of enormous integrity, but he would trust the leadership to create its own style of action.

When he retired in 1984, he received the ACPE Distinguished Service Award. ACPE is greatly indebted to Charles Hall for writing *Head and Heart,* his perspective on the movement and ACPE.

The next choice for Executive Director was Duane Parker. Duane had been at the Topeka State Hospital prior to his move to the Interfaith Health Care Ministries in Providence, RI. He had been a regional director In the South Central Region and was active on many national committees prior to his selection. Duane served from 1984 through May 1994.

Duane was also described accurately by James Gebhart:

> Administrator, communicator, friend, adversary, advocate, and theologian, sensitive soul –which was Duane... He was devoted to and absolutely respectful of his predecessor. Yet he immediately reshaped the central office in its new Decatur location with his own personality and values. It was to become a place of friendship, openness, candor, appreciation, inquiry, diligence, and trust When he chose Helen Patton to be his colleague, ACPE entered an era of unprecedented grace and hospitality. And, he absolutely trusted that ACPE leadership was forthcoming from many different sources. And so it was not surprising that with Duane, the Association literally leaped forward with new energy, optimism and focus. (p. 5.)

Duane Parker was credited with vision and with the ability to empower creative people to take leadership challenges. He personally was interested in international outreach and conferences. He was very involved and worked very coopera-tively with other cognate groups.

A comparison of Hall's leadership style with that of Duane Parker's was easy to observe at the Annual Meetings. At the Conference, Hall would always sit at the Officer's table and would, when asked, intersperse the history of a particular problem or policy or policy recommendation. This provided very valuable information. Parker, on the other hand, would be out in the audience at official General Assembly and Annual Meetings but always responded when asked. Hall's refusal or inability to write down policies of past Board meetings for an incoming president frustrated this writer! Unwritten precedents, if not written down, could not be debated; Hall's memory of policy issues often prevailed!

Parker had no public crisis like the 1976 House of Delegates' meeting where the Executive Committee's decision to employ an Associate Director failed, but he did have occasional difficulties. Parker ably represented ACPE, took an active and important part in the cooperative planning and at meetings with other national and international groups.

When Parker returned to Interfaith in Providence, Helen Patton was named interim Executive Director. She provided important leadership for ACPE during a time of leadership transition. Previously she had served as an Administrator and was highly regarded by the membership.

The Rev. Dr. Russell Davis, Supervisor at the University of Virginia Health Sciences Center, Charlottesville, VA, was selected to be the next Executive Director. Russell was not widely known outside his region. He came to the ACPE with a concern to bring it more fully into the computer and internet age.

> Coming in during a time of transition and change Russell has helped us begin the process to be more fully automated in the national office (thus eliminating the hand-filing of the yellow cards) which is not an easy task. He has been instrumental in assisting to create the National Interfaith Coalition, as well as working with the Joint Commission to be more attuned to the standards for Spiritual Care. Long hours were put in by Russell to keep our accreditation with the US Dept. of Education.
>
> We wish you well. (ACPE News. September-October, 1998. Vol. XXXI. p. 2.)

One of the officers at that time said that Russell had done a superb work in the re-recognition process. Missed expectations, however, led to Dr. Davis' resignation in July of 1998

The Board of Representatives reviewed the ACPE needs that summer and called a full-time Interim Office Administrator, Mrs.

Nancy Parker, and a part-time interim Executive Director, Rev. Stuart Plummer, South Central Regional Director, who commuted from Fraser, Colorado. They began their duties on October 5, 1998 and have served very effectively through March of 2000.

In the meantime, the Board's Personnel Committee presented The Rev. Gary Sartain, The Good Samaritan Society, St. Paul, and The Rev. Teresa Snorton, Director of the Emory Center for Pastoral Services, a major ACPE accredited center in Atlanta as its nominees. Rev. Teresa Snorton was selected. She had also been serving as Chair of the Racial Ethnic Multicultural Network. She began her duties on February 14, 2000 for a period of not less than three nor more than five years, with an option to renew. (ACPE News. January-February, 2000. p. 33.)

THE PRESIDENTS
(See Appendix II for a list of Presidents and their terms, beginning with 1968).

Since 1992, several of the former Presidents have responded with 2-12 pages of reflections on their presidency and two have videotaped their reflections, which are available in the ACPE office and at the ACPE Archives at Pitts Theology Library.

Ideally, this history should intertwine their accomplishments with the many changes documented herein and their leadership roles in so many of them should be identified. Neither the author's time nor skill was able to accomplish that task. That opportunity remains for another.

FINANCES

The yearly membership fees in 1967 were set at Centers: $200.00; Supervisors: $25.00; student fees: $5.00. Seminaries, denominations, and Council of Churches were also charged a yearly fee.

The next year, a successful campaign was launched to secure individual memberships and to spread the ACPE story to the public. Supervisors responded well to requests for names of potential members. Membership fees were set at $15.00, including the Journal of Pastoral Care (JPC) and $10.00 without the JPC. Life memberships were available at $1,000.00, which could be paid over 10 years. Total gifts in the first 6 months were $20,032.01, including 320 Supervisors and 688 general members. (ACCPE News. July, 1968. Vol. 1, No. 7. p. 2.)

By December 1968, there were 2,000 founding members including six life members. At the same time, the Stone Foundation provided a matching grant to assist the development project of the Journal of Pastoral Care to mail 3,000 copies of the JPC to potential customers.

By 1968, ACPE had a year-end balance of $6,969.00, but with a warning from the Treasurer (the first of several warnings throughout the years) that fees would have to be raised, expenses reduced, or other sources of income be found. The next year the Treasurer, Richard Wittrip, a hospital adminis-trator, reported a more favorable balance than last year.

Since serving God had turned out to be such a rewarding event, we wanted to avoid unexpectedly finding ourselves responding solely to mammon. (ACPE News. November, 1970. Vol. III, No. 11. p. 2.)

This good news enabled a 1971 budget to be set at $127,500.00 and the situation remained good until 1975. Treasurer Lloyd reported a projected deficit of $10,000.00 for that year. There was also no increase in the number of centers during the general economic recession, as there had been in previous years. (ACPE News. 1975. Vol. VIII, No. 9-10. p. 2.)

Concerns about national versus regional fees was one of the issues which led to the 1976 Special Study Committee report to the House in 1977.

The ACPE has had several successful financial campaigns throughout the following years. One began in 1983 to meet the Kresge Challenge Grant of $75,000.00 which ACPE would receive if it would receive five year pledges of over $108,000.00 to pay off the mortgage on the two Decatur office condos. That goal was met.

Another fund-raising event was the Caring Choice goal of $100,000.00 to fund the Design for the 80's. In all of these campaigns, supervisors as individuals and their regions gave generously.

In 1999, the office in Decatur was cleaned and painted, old furniture was replaced and the computer system was upgraded.

Here again, the regions have come through with substantial pledges, though the approximately $100,000.00 immediate cost was taken from the endowment fund, to be repaid on a yearly basis with the pledge payments assisting.

In the discussion of finances, the predecessor organizations owe a real debt to the W. Clement and Jessie Stone Foundation for a grant of nearly $97,500.00 so that CCT and IPC Supervisors could meet in joint planning committees and at joint conferences to speed up the merger negotiations. Mr. Stone received the First ACPE Appreciation Award in 1990.

Twenty year financial comparisons are listed below:

	1978	**1998**	**1999**
		(Audited)	(Preliminary)
Income*	691,935	880,490	772,635
Expenses*	621,570	985,383	826,705
Net change*	70,365	(104,893)	(54,070)
Endowment Fund*	358,923	1,228,674	1,448,646

Other Assets include the office condos in Decatur, GA.

This does not include the financial reports of the 9 Regions with combined assets of over $1,100.000. Regions are now a part of the ACPE incorporated as 501 (c)(3).

DENOMINATIONS/FAITH GROUP AND SUPERVISOR RELATIONSHIPS

Practically all the CPE supervisors in the early years were in chaplaincy positions. Except for World War II, when the military required endorsements for its chaplains, many of the denominations had no system of ecclesiastical endorsement. The heavy demand by institutions for chaplains literally took off, to the surprise of most everyone. Denominations began to develop procedures for identifying chaplains and endorsing them, either through a national process, or leaving that to the area jurisdictions, depending upon denominational polity. For example, the Presbyterian Church in 1956 finally established an Office of Institutional Chaplaincy under its Board of National Missions. This was done at the instigation of chaplains!

Each denomination set its own standards for recognition, standards to meet for denominational endorsement. Many denominations required a minimum of three years of parish experience and so that standard was included in the normal requirements for certification as a Supervisor.

While the Supervisor in the institution was still ultimately accountable to her/his own denomination, the Supervisor was directly accountable to the institution's Director, Superintendent or Clinical Director. Now instead of being directly responsible to only one ecclesiastical authority, whether it is to the local parish board, or a bishop or a denominational agency, chaplains, and others in non-parish ministries were now accountable to institutional hierarchies of power.

Although in the beginning, chaplains in general hospitals were mainly in church institutions, the secular governmental and non-profit institutions saw the value of chaplains and an increasing number of positions opened up. Sometimes denominations and interdenominational agencies even took the lead in funding positions in public institutions. They also provided scholarship assistance for clergy who needed to have clinical pastoral education to qualify for such positions. In other denominations, would-be chaplains had to fend for themselves and actually organized groups, e.g. The Presbyterian Association for Specialized Pastoral Ministries, which included chaplains, supervisors and pastoral counselors, before having some impact on the denominational agencies.

Ecclesiastical endorsement for chaplaincy positions varied all the way from being listed on a page in the annual clergy roster to meeting a denominational committee before one could even proceed toward chaplaincy and supervisory CPE. For many there was a formal denominational and/or faith group review before one was endorsed.

By the time of the merger in 1967, ACPE leaders recognized that more structured relationships with the denominations were needed. A category of denominational agency membership was established and six denominational representatives were included in the House of Delegates. There were between ten and twelve denominational agencies as members of ACPE.

By the time of the Special Study Committee report in 1980 it wrote:

> During the years of ACPE, CPE Supervisors have been in dialogue with denominational agencies. Although the

relationship has sometimes been an adversary relationship, it has moved toward becoming one of cooperation. (Special Study Committee Report. p. 16-17.)

It must be remembered that it took an unusual clergyperson to move into the psychiatric hospitals prior to WWII. Some were rebels within their denominations and had a love-hate relationship with those who had ordained them.

Among the recommendations of The Special Study Committee were some of the following:

> Continuation of the denominational agency category;
> The General Assembly shall have one denominational representative from each participating denomination;
> The Board of Representatives shall have a Denominational Advisory Council;
> The Commission on Certification and the Commission on Accreditation (COMISS) shall have denominational representatives as members;
> ACPE shall continue its active participation in the Council on Ministries in Specialized Settings. (p. 17.)

It also made similar proposals to the regions and the centers to involve denominations at the local levels. (p. 18.)

These proposals were adopted. Annual ACPE Conferences continued to have a special place where supervisors and denominational executives could breakfast together. Denominational executives also continued to play an active role in the affairs of COMISS. The decision to delay the timing of the Dialogue meeting of all pastoral care, counseling and education organizations was made so that the denominations could get involved and thus also could claim ownership. (Hall, C. 1981. Personal Communication; Hall, C. 1992. p. 209.)

One of the high points of denominational-ACPE relationships was at the Dialogue '88 meeting when the denominational executives signed the COMISS agreement, making it a Congress instead of a Council.

Many supervisors feel supported by their denominations while some would like more recognition and appreciation for their unique ACPE ministry. Today some individual denominations are having their own crises, sometimes because of doctrinal and governance issues and the resulting financial pressures or for other reasons because of budgets and downsizing. Even some parish pastors are feeling unsupported by their denominational leaders because of the many changes taking place within the denominations. Some denominations have reported increased overall giving but more of it is going to local and regional causes and less funding is going to national causes.

SEMINARY RELATIONSHIPS

Both the CCT and the IPC needed the seminaries to provide students for their programs. At the same time, they were trying to change seminary education. In the early years, Episcopal Seminaries at Alexandria, Virginia, Cambridge, Massachusetts, and Philadelphia, and seminaries in the Boston area and the Chicago Theological Seminary (CTS) were the key supporters of CPE. They were willing to trust their students to the CCT and the IPC. CTS put Anton T. Boisen on its faculty. Baptist seminaries in Louisville and Winston-Salem and Lutheran Seminaries in Columbia, South Carolina, Philadelphia and St. Paul were among keys to the development in the Association of Clinical Pastoral Educators (primarily Baptist) and the Lutheran Advisory Committee. The IPC was a consortium of seminaries and training centers in the Boston area in which the seminaries had special responsibilities. The CCT had seminary members but while some seminary representatives were on its Board, the seminaries were less influential comparedwith the IPC.

In the Southwest, The Council of Southwestern Theological Seminaries (COSTS) began a special relationship with an independent program, the Institute of Religion in Houston in the middle 1950's and beyond.

The CPE relationships with the core theological disciplines in the seminaries was ambiguous in earlier years. The Practical Fields were more receptive to CPE and its supervisors had good relationships with the professors of pastoral care and counseling and the seminary field education programs as these positions developed in the 1950's and 1960's. The graduate school programs produced the professors in this field: Paul Johnson at Boston University School of Theology; Seward Hiltner at the University of Chicago's Divinity School; Carroll Wise at Garrett Biblical Institute (now Seminary); and Howard Clinebell at Claremont School of Theology, produced the majority of the professors in these fields. Several programs required CPE of their doctoral candidates. Supervisors who only ran summer units were quite dependent upon the seminaries for their students. One denominational representative recently informed the writer that his denomination required CPE for ordination and thus about 1,500 students per year were placed in CPE programs.

Placement of students was originally the function of the central offices and the Supervisors. By the time of the formation of ACPE applications were routed directly to the center of first choice, and sometimes students submitted applications to more than one center, creating problems for the supervisors. One of the seminary complaints has been the delay in holding on to applications so those students didn't know whether or not they had been accepted. Another complaint was the delay in getting the admissions interview to the center of first choice..

The delay in getting the Supervisor's report back to the seminary has also been a problem area. Originally the CCT supervisors wrote one report which was sent to the seminary and it was carefully written to avoid any of the Supervisor's interpretation of personality dynamics. The other report to the CCT was more candid and evaluative in the event the student applied for further training. By the time of the merger that practice had ceased. Supervisors began writing more descriptive reports and left it up to the reader to evaluate it. The question of the ownership of the Supervisor's evaluation of the student was unclear for many years, but more recently the decision was finally made that the report belonged to the student. It is up to the student to release it to whom ever she/he desired. If the student was receiving academic credit, then some form of report or grade was due at the academic institution.

Students have been asked to identify the learning goals for the particular unit, before or just after the unit begins. The student then is accountable to the supervisor for reviewing, revising and completing his/her learning goals for the particular unit. In most programs, the student's final evaluation seminar was the time when the student shared his/her own with report with her/his peers, the supervisors. Sometimes one or more members of the unit staff were invited in for part of the session. Supervisors demystify their reports by reminding the students that the report is based on a description of the student's functioning in relation to the chosen goals. Nothing esoteric is going on.

The Special Study Committee recommended the formation of a Committee on Theological Schools. A later change has created a Seminary Advisory Council which insures that one representative of the Council would be on the ACPE Board and could even serve even on its Executive Committee.

One of the ways that the relationship between ACPE and the regions has been fostered was through the establishment of Regional Committees on Theological Education. Such Committees serve a variety of functions including engaging in research projects, arranging for dialogue between supervisors and professors, providing opportunities for discussing changes in both CPE and theological education, and exploring ways to increase the cooperation between ACPE and the seminaries.

A number of supervisors have pursued and earned the degree of D. Min. from seminaries. This has led to closer relationships between individual supervisors and specific seminaries, and this has been helpful to the movement and to ACPE.

SEMINARY ADVISORY COUNCIL

The current Chair is J. Paul Balas of Lutheran Seminary at Gettysburg, and his able predecessors were Otto Bucher of Sacred Heart Seminary, Hales Corners, WI, and Jack White of Lutheran Theological Seminary, Philadelphia.

This group meets only at Annual Conferences and attendance varies between three and twenty-five. It elects one representative to the Board of Representatives. A number of the long-term seminary professors have retired. This means that with only yearly meetings there is less time to develop the relationships, which had previously occurred. As they gather, they report candid discussions. Some of them meet together at regional meetings. The seminary professors in the practical fields have their own professional groups, the Society for Pastoral Theology and the International Academy of Practical Theology..

The special relationship of the Association of Theological Schools (ATS) began at the time of the 50th Anniversary of ACPE in 1975 when the Readiness for Ministry Study was presented at the conference by Merton Strommen. David Schuller of ATS developed a specially designed instrument for ACPE, which was discussed in the section on Research.

In 1967, no Roman Catholic Seminaries belonged to any of the predecessor organizations. In August, 1969 the Field Education Directors of those seminaries held a consultation with representatives of ACPE at Georgetown University. Some regions made it possible for their Roman Catholic supervisors to attend that meeting. (ACPE News. 1969. Vol. II, No. 9&10. p. 2.) After that meeting, there were soon twenty-seven Roman Catholic member seminaries. Today there are twenty-one such seminaries which belong. Father Joseph Hornacek, from St. Francis Seminary in Milwaukee, Wisconsin, and who had taken a unit of CPE, was elected ACPE Secretary in the late 1970's.

In addition, nine seminaries not related to the main line denominations are members, as well as three Jewish Theological Institutions which are now members, one with three separate campuses.

There has been on very rare occasion the need to inform ACPE about a situation which needs correcting. They feel positive about ACPE and its educational programs. Their new representative to the Board was very impressed with their functioning at the 1999 Board meeting he attended.

CLINICAL MEMBERS ADVISORY COUNCIL

This new category came into existence as a result of the Special Study Committee. There was considerable discussion in the Committee; one of the arguments was that we ought to get feedback from the users of our services, the Chaplains. This category of membership would accomplish that as they participated in regional and national conferences. The question as to whether or not they should be certified proved troublesome. The plan was for clinical members to be active members of the Association, have at least two units of basic and two units of Advanced CPE and to pay a membership fee, initially $50.00 per year and now currently $110.00 per year.

Approximately 1,400 became clinical members, qualifying on the basis of four or more units recognized by ACPE. The proposal to certify clinical members was a real threat by the chaplaincy organizations and was dropped. Clinical members have met together in some regions at the time of regional meetings and at the national meetings. Some serve on regional committees.

In 1986, clinical members questioned the Board about their role in ACPE. In 1988, a Task Force, chaired by Janet Brown, was established. In 1993, a clinical member breakfast was held in Louisville, Kentucky. In 1996, the Board established the Clinical

Member Advisory Council and Janet Brown was the first representative to the Board in 1997. The current representative is Irvin Moore, Jr., who reports a survey done in 1999 will be published in an upcoming ACPE News. The current number of clinical members is approximately 643. (Moore, I. February 25, 2000. Personal Communication.)

Current governance states:

> The Clinical Members Advisory Council shall meet each year at the ACPE Annual Conference and will serve in an advisory capacity to the Board on matters of interest to Clinical Members. All members who attend the annual meeting shall be members. A Chairperson who has been recommended to RANC to be nominated for a three-year term. The chairperson cannot succeed her/ himself. (Governance Manual. Revised May, 1997. p. 9.)

RESEARCH

Dr. Boisen was basically a researcher seeking to understand his own and the religious dimensions of non-organic mental illness. He had an inquiring mind and he had an inductive approach to problems. He was willing to ask questions and receive help from people in a wide variety of professional fields.

His studies of the "living human documents" in the hospital and in the community were published in both books and in a variety of journals, including prominent psychiatric journals, e.g. American Journal of Psychiatry, PSYCHIATRY, and the Journal of Clinical Psychology. (Boison, A. 1960. *Out of The Depths.* Harper. p. 211-216.) They were also published in religious journals. (Boisen, A. and Asquith. *Readings From an Unknown Country.*)

The prior organizations were also willing to study what they were doing. The ACPE initial structure provided for a Research Committee. Many of the supervisors had studied for advanced degrees in seminaries and universities which required theses, sometimes involving clinical studies.

But Powell was correct in 1975, asking the question, *Whatever happened to religious research?* The partial answer was through its Research Committee and its participation in the Joint Council on Research. But most of the research was applied research, rather than basic research. An altogether too brief a review of the ABSTRACTS and a review of Dr. Robert Fuller's "Rediscovering The Laws of Spiritual Life: The Last Twenty Years of Supervision and Training in Ministry" (to be published in a forthcoming issue of JSTM) shows a pragmatic focus on how to do better training, counseling and ministry. The inductive method has focused primarily on questions having to do with applying our efforts toward becoming better practitioners and educators. The time and funds required for basic research into human personality and the function of religious beliefs and spiritual and mystical understandings are not readily available to working chaplains, counselors and educators.

Tests have been utilized to measure the outcomes of spiritual care In hospitals. Several attempts have been made to develop "Spiritual Assessment" instruments to assist chaplains in identifying the most needy patients. These are both key needs for those supervising CPE students in their ministry to patients. The Joint Commission on the Accreditation of Hospitals (JACOAH) surveyors are now more concerned with the outcomes of care given. Simply checking the credentials of staff providing it is no longer sufficient. Outcome studies and spiritual assessment studies are critical and require our best research efforts. (Derrickson, P. February 6, 2000. Personal Communication.)

George A. Fitchett reports:

> In 1990, Paul Derrickson published a review of studies of changes which resulted from CPE. (JPC. 1990. Vol. 44) Reviewing 136 articles he found thirty-nine studies that employed standardized instruments to assess three broad changes in CPE students. Studies that examined changes in basic character or personality found little change as a result of CPE. Studies which examined changes in values and attitudes often yielded significant results. Those changes were generally in the direction of greater autonomy and sensitivity to self and others. The third group of studies examined changes in interpersonal relations and in general the results have been measurable and positive.
>
> In 1983, the Clinical Ministry Assessment Profile (CMAP) was offered to CPE supervisors. The ACPE Research Committee in conjunction with the Association of Theological Schools (ATS) developed this instrument...

While the CMAP did not become popular with supervisors, it afforded important possibilities for studying the outcomes of CPE programs using a comprehensive, carefully developed measure of professional functioning. Fitchett and colleagues have conducted two studies of the outcomes of CPE using the CMAP. In the first study (Fitchett and Gray. 1994. Journal of Supervision and Training in Ministry), they studied thirty-three students who completed one year of CPE. They found substantial, positive changes in the student's pre- versus post-CPE CMAP scores. All CMAP sub-scales showed changes in the desired direction and for ten of the sub-scales, the changes were statistically significant. In the second study, presented at the 1996 annual meeting, they examined changes in a national sample of 203 studies who completed a basic unit of CPE. Again, they found substantial, positive changes in the desired direction in both the students' self-ratings as well as in the supervisors' ratings of the students. Taken together, these two studies provide important evidence of the positive outcomes of professional performance that result from CPE. (Fitchett, G. March 9, 2000. Personal Communication.)

George Fitchett and Larry VandeCreek are among the out-standing contemporary researchers among ACPE supervisors.

Some Supervisors, like James Gibbons when at the University of Chicago Hospitals, have built research requirements into their residency programs.

INTERORGANIZATIONAL RELATIONSHIPS

ACPE itself is a result of an interorganizational relationship between four groups. Once the merger took place, there have been many voices and opportunities within ACPE seeking closer relationships among the pastoral care, counseling and education organizations. A number of active supervisors have been and continue to belong to more than one group. They include the American Association of Pastoral Counselors (AAPC) and many were active in its organization in 1963. A number of supervisors were very active in the formation of the College of Chaplains (COC) of the American Protestant Hospital Association in 1946. The same was true for the Association of Mental Health Chaplains (AMHC) in 1948. The AMHC organized the first interfaith certification process which included Jewish, Protestant and Roman Catholic chaplains in 1968. (This writer was AMHC President that year.) These latter two groups merged as the Association of Professional Chaplains (APC) in 1998. Fewer supervisors were involved with the American Correctional Chaplains' Association (ACCA) and one of its subsidiary groups, The American Protestant Correctional Chaplains Association (APCCA) organized in 1950. The National Association of Catholic Chaplains (NACC) was organized in 1965 but in later years has a good number of ACPE-certified priests and sisters in its ranks. A joint APC-NACC conference was held in early 2000. William Gaventa has been in a more recent leadership position with the Religion Division of the American Association of Mental Deficiency, (AAMD) formed in 1965. The National Association of Business and Industrial Chaplains (NIBIC) was formed in 1970. The latest chaplaincy organization is the National Association of Jewish Chaplains (NAJC) which began participating in the Journal of Pastoral Care (JPC) in 1992.

The Canadian Association for Pastoral Education (CAPE) was founded after seeing the American divisions among the pastoral care groups. There has been joint recognition of supervisory status from time to time between CAPE and ACPE and cordial relationships with the presidents routinely visiting each other's annual conferences. One joint meeting was held in Detroit in 1976 with the late Henri Nouwen as the main speaker.

At one time or another ACPE has held official relationships with several other professional organizations in the health field. The primary initial interorganizational cooperation has been the publication of The Journal of Pastoral Care (JPC) which began in 1948 after the CCT and the IPC each published the first issue of their new journals. The Journal has its own Board which manages the Journal, including the employment of the Editor and Business Management. Luberta McCabe was the first editor, serving for 24 years, and Orlo Strunk has now served for 18 years. The ACPE office has provided the business management functions. The Journal has had its own Editorial Committee which establishes editorial policies and reviews manuscripts. This Board consists of representatives from each of the current participating groups: the APC, ACPE, CAPPE (formerly CAPE), APC, NAJC and NIBIC. The history of the movement could also be told through the pages of the Journal since 1948.

Joint Conferences have been held with AAPC in 1971, 1972 and 1999 and more recently with COC and AMHC in 1998 at Portland, Oregon at the time of those two groups' merger into APC. The APC and the NACC met jointly in Charlotte, North Carolina in 2000.

The Central Region of AAPC and the North Central Region of the ACPE jointly sponsored the publication of the Journal of Supervision and Training in Ministry (JSTM) in 1979. It has been self-sustaining since its start and celebrated its 20th Anniversary in 1999.

In 1971, the College of Chaplains set up an interorganizational consultation and a representative of the Department of Religion and Medicine of the American Medical Association participated, as well as ACPE and other cognate groups. Those consultations continued on an interorganizational basis for several years.

In 1977, the desire for more cooperation between the religious endorsing bodies and the pastoral organizations led in 1978-79 to the formation of the Council on Ministry in Specialized Settings (COMISS). It was open to all groups and to all denominations/faith groups. COMISS meets annually, sponsors a national ecumenical Pastoral Care Week each Fall, and is the main vehicle of cooperation between the religious endorsing groups and the pastoral care, counseling and education groups. A COMISS accreditation program which evaluates the chaplaincy/pastoral/spiritual care departments of hospitals is called the Joint Accreditation of Pastoral Services (JACAPS). It is available to hospitals who wish to have their programs evaluated. The Rev. Wazz Raff (APC) and the late Sister Helen Hayes (NACC) have been two of the pioneers in initiating this accreditation service.

The Joint Council on Research in Pastoral Care and Counseling (JCRPCC) idea began in 1970. It was organized in 1972 and published its first Annual Abstracts in 1972 (Vol. 2. p. ii-iii.) It, too, was a joint cooperative effort of several cognate organizations and continues today. (1982. Vol. 12. p. ii-vi.)

The Special Study Committee of ACPE in its 1980 report had looked at the other organizations carefully, had come up with an idea of an Academy of Pastoral Care. The report encouraged further efforts toward a federation of organizations. The Joint Issues in Pastoral Care Organizations (JIPCO) consisting of the Presidents and Executives of the several groups was formed in

1980. JIPCO also encouraged a joint meeting of all of the organizations as early as 1983 or 1984. Several Executives delayed any actions by COMISS until the denominational representatives could claim some ownership. (Hall. p. 209.) After much careful work and planning Dialogue '88 was held in Minneapolis with over 1,000 members of the several cognate groups in attendance. At that meeting religious endorsing agents of many faith groups/denominations along with those from the cognate groups signed the charter of the new Congress of Ministries in Specialized Settings. It was a stirring conference but almost too full, as each group had its annual meetings as well as the main program events.

A second follow-up Dialogue was held in Milwaukee in 1994 with an equally good turnout. COMISS has recently dropped its Georgia incorporation in favor of Wisconsin, and has decided to become a Network and to have its office at NACC in Milwaukee. There are no immediate plans for another Dialogue.

In 1996, a National Interfaith Coalition for Spiritual Healthcare and Counseling (NICSH) was organized as the latest cooperative effort. This is an attempt to focus and bring the message of the movement's contributions to spiritual care to the larger and more influential important audiences. It started with a great media meeting at the National Press Club in Washington with prominent politicians and health care leaders present on September 18, 1997.

Each state was to organize its own interfaith coalition, and some states did that, e.g. New Jersey with its annual conference on October 4, 1999. (East by Northeast. Winter, 2000. Vol. 27, No. 1. p. 4) But for a variety of reasons, including the $10,000.00 annual fee, both the ACPE and the APC had given, they both decided to terminate their relationship with NICSH. It was perceived as not meeting ACPE's needs and therefore was not considered a good stewardship of ACPE's limited resources.

William Baugh's CPE Presidential Inaugural Address in 1996 was titled *Call to Partnership*. It was an open letter to the Presidents or Presidents-elect of the other cognate groups. President Baugh invited them to participate in a visioning conference toward an increasing partnership. (ACPE News. August-September, 1996. Vol. XXIX, No. 4. p. 1.) His presidential colleagues responded positively and that initiative has blossomed. In 1997, the Fall Meeting of the Board approved

$9,000.00 out of unused foundation grant funds to finance ACPE's continued participation in this effort.

John Moody has been selected as the convenor of the Collaborative Steering Committee. This is his report:

> AMHC (later COC and AMHC merged to form APC) was presented to a meeting of the Boards of the respective organizations in Nashville, November 1998. ACPE, APC and NACC were represented by their full Boards of Directors. AAPC was represented by its Executive Committee..., led to the formation of a Steering Committee with up to three representatives from each organization. The group was charged with developing a collaborative model for the several organizations that was cost effective, preserved the value of the many pastoral care specialties, and further developed the pastoral care, counseling and education movement in the USA. John Moody, David Carl and Joan Hemenway were selected by the ACPE Board to be its representatives. Joan had to decline the position and Maxine Glaz was appointed in her place. The group appointed three representatives to carry on this process. It is now called the Collaborative Steering Committee. At recent meetings, it proposed to come up with a preliminary report of an operating model for a second conjoint meeting of the Boards of Directors again in Nashville, November 2000... if the Boards affirm the work of the Committee, with a goal of providing a model and transitional plan by the end of 2001. (Moody, J. February 17, 2000. Personal Communication.)

If so, the many years of interorganizational cooperation will make sense to those who have given so many, many hours and even more energy to bring it about.

INTERNATIONAL COOPERATIVE EFFORTS

The modern pastoral care, education and counseling movement has been blessed with the number of students from other lands coming to our shores for further education and training. In turn, our leaders have been invited to conferences in other lands, and have been asked to provide on-site training in CPE and pastoral counseling for periods from several weeks to one year in places as far removed as Africa, India, Japan, the Philippines and

Singapore as well as Europe. Our supervisors have responded with enthusiasm to such requests. This story deserves a separate history.

In a joint conferences in July 1972 in Arnoldshain, West Germany and in July of 1975 at Ruschilkon, Switzerland, a cooperative desire developed for an International Congress on Pastoral Care and Counseling. The first Congress was held in Edinburgh in 1979; the next in San Francisco in 1983; in Melbourne in 1987; in Noordwijkerhout, The Netherlands in 1991; in Toronto, Canada in 1995; and in Accra, Ghana in 1999.

While not an official cooperative effort, the formation of the Pastoral Care Network for Social Responsibility in 1984 enabled that group to meet at each subsequent annual ACPE Conference and at the International Congress meetings. The International Pastoral Care Network for Social Responsibility formally organize at the 1991 Congress in Holland. Howard Clinebell has been the prime mover in this effort, which started out focused on the Nuclear Issue but now has broadened into Earth Keeping. It publishes a quarterly NEWSLETTER and has a web page, www.ipcnsr.org.

ENROLLMENT CATEGORY STUDENT TRENDS: 1986-1996

A comparison of the categories of the students enrolled in ACPE units between 1988 and 1996 is as follows: The total number of units provided, 6894, gained 235 units (3%). Over 30% of student units are taken by seminarians and the next largest category is by parish clergy (20%). Institutional chaplains follow at 16%. Lay persons totaled 916 or nearly 15% of the 6984 total units provided.

The number of seminary units decreased 140 units (2%) from 2179 to 2039. The number of parish pastors units shows an 8% decline from 1532 to 1396 units. The number of institutional chaplains shows an increase of 147 (18%) from 814 to 961. Military chaplains' units declined from 245 to 174 units, a loss of 71 (29%). Missionaries constituted a small group, declining from 46 to 31, a loss of 15 (29%). Graduate student units dropped from 383 to 372, only 11%. Foreign students' units showed a gain from 194 to 273, 79 (40%); Religious orders declined from 451 to 406 units, 45 (10%). The Other category, gained 75 units, 276 to 351 (27%).

What category of student units showed an increase to make up for the several declining categories? The number of units by lay persons increased quite significantly from 629 in 1988 to 981 in 1996, an increase of 352 (56%)! While statistics from more recent years are not available, conversations with contemporary supervisors indicates a continuation of this trend. It is anticipated that the figures for laypersons will be even higher in later years. Some centers which provide extended unit opportunities have seen an increase in their enrollments by a number of lay pastoral care persons, both men and women.

During the same period, percentage figures show a continuing increase in the percentage of women students. 1996 showed a shift to 51% men and 49% women, nearly an 8% increase above the 58% male units and 42% women's units in 1988. Of the 981 (15%) lay persons' units, 225 (25%) were men and 691 (75%) were women. (ACPE News. September, 1987. Vol. XXII, No. 4. p. 9; ACPE News. December, 1997. Vol. XXX, No. 6. p. 3.)

SURVEY OF SENIOR SUPERVISORS

Thomas sent out 145 non-randomized questionnaires in July, 1999, to experienced supervisors who had been in ACPE for twenty to thirty years and were known to him. Forty-four of them responded (a return rate of 30%) to YOUR EVALUATION OF CHANGES IN CPE, a series of nine questions. (Thomas, J. 1999. Unpublished Survey.)

Supervisors sent in carefully thought out answers with personal examples and vignettes. It is regrettable not to have enough room to print many of their responses. It was possible to have more than one response to a question so percentages may add to more than 100%!

Question 1: Any changes in the motivation of and goals of students seeking CPE? Thirty-five percent identified a more professional motivation, 21% saw no significant changes; 11% felt the students were less motivated, or, for some seminary students, taking it because it was required. Eleven percent saw more personal motivations, whereas only 7% identified the students as being more motivated. Here is one quote:

..."Mid-life" seminarians... have convictions of what the church and parishioner should not expect of them... in this group there is little "awe" of the office of ordained ministry... They want techniques for hospital ministry and lists of things to do or say, and are resistant to "pastoral formation" questions or groups.

The second question had to do with any changes in the types of students compared with those in much earlier years. Thirty-seven percent identified the students as older and the same percentage identified more women students. Thirty-three percent were second career students and there were increases in the percentages of international students, more Roman Catholic students, more gay and lesbian students, more theologically conservative students, more lay persons, more non-Christian . Fourteen percent were identified as more troubled students. One spoke for many: "many more women entering professional life for the first time."

Question 3. How have changes in the settings influenced your programs? has already been discussed in a previous section. But, as one supervisor put it after supervising for 30 years in several types of settings:

> The primary change has been the proliferation of professionals doing the same work. Things I once did as a chaplain, and therefore my students were called upon to do, are increasingly addressed by other professionals... Also, we have doctors and nurses who want to work with patients around "spiritual issues," but don't want to deal with any religious content or consult with the chaplain unless the patient demands it, or they get into trouble...

Question 4 addressed the original source of the Supervisor's satisfaction over the years. Are there any changes in the source of your satisfaction in latter years? Seventy-nine percent of the Supervisors find satisfaction as the students are eager to grow and change, 23% find it harder to find satisfaction and 16% see no change in their level of satisfaction.

Question 5 has to do with the level of Supervisors' participation in regional and sub-regional meetings and any changes through the years. Fifty-one percent report less activity, 32.5% maintain the same level as in the past, only 7% are more active, and 16% indicated that they were retired.

Question 6 asks the same question as No. 5 except in reference to regional and national conferences. Here, again, is an unmistakable change. Forty-four percent report less activity, 11% cannot go because of time and financial constraints, 25% find no change in the level of their activity, 9% go for fellowship and a similar number are retired, while only 7% report more participation in regional and national meetings.

Question 7. As standards and accreditation and certification guidelines and procedures have changed over the years, what changes have been helpful and which have been of little use or detrimental in your program? Forty-four percent said the changes had been helpful, 32.5% said the changes had been less helpful, 18% replied the changes had been too frequent and 11% said the changes had limited creativity. Over 44% indicated that CPE needs reform.

Question 8 asked whether supervisors had been aware of changes in the religious/spiritual aspects of their supervision with students in recent years? A wide variety of comments surfaced here, among them:

Increasing spiritual direction notions have made positive impact on supervision.

Student's theology and call as important as personal awareness now. Before, it was an insight and no revelations.

See a greater interest in traditional spirituality as regard to prayer and singing as we are seeing more students with conservative backgrounds. Simple ministry is still a high priority, especially with first quarter students. (Davis, J.)

Now I intentionally incorporate spiritual and theological in supervision and in programs. Another example is that we have an overnight Covenant retreat at the mid-point of each unit... This is often a turning point for CPE students. (Parker, D.)

This has always been an important dimension in my supervision and still is... what has kept me growing in my work and personhood. (Lehman, R.)

Absolutely –I feel more focused on this dimension than when I started. I have made an effort to integrate more spirituality into my programs. (Silberman, J.)

Sixty percent indicated they had been aware of the changes they had made; 16% indicated that students were less critical and more conservative; 9% were more aware of ecumenical concerns; and 7% were unaware of any significant changes.

Question 9 asked for changes in relationship with any of the following:

a. Denomination or faith group. Thirty-nine percent report the same, 18% reported more relationships, 14% decreased, and 30% did not answer the question.

b. Theological seminaries. Sixty-one percent reported no change, 14% reported increased relationships, and the same percentage was reported for decreased relationships.

In relationships with other cognate groups (e.g. AAPC, APC, etc.) 55% indicated no change.

Smaller increases and decreases were indicated for both AAPC and APC, and two indicated a relationship with College of Supervision and Supervision in Pastoral Psychotherapy.

Any changes in the use of JOURNAL OF PASTORAL CARE? Sixty-eight percent indicated no changes, 7% used it less and 7% used it more frequently.

ACPE Network activity. Only 20% related to networks and only a few networks were listed by name once or twice: Research, International, Public Issues, Peace, History. This leads to the probable conclusion that the Networks involve more younger Supervisors.

SUPERVISORS, LITERATURE AND ACPE WEBPAGE
www.acpe.edu

Appendix I indicates a supervisor's library prior to 1960. Since then, the field has burgeoned, with books almost too numerous to list, and with journals in related fields. The JPC itself has published fourteen Books and Journals and seven Monographs. (JPC Publications. Decatur, GA.)

Supervisors and former Supervisors who are teaching in seminaries have produced abundant literature, which could be a separate publication on its own. That is another task remaining to be done.

ACPE has its own webpage, www.acpe.edu, with an extensive Table of Contents of thirteen items. It even includes the minutes of Board meetings!

STRATEGIC PLANNING

The Board created a Strategic Coordinating Committee with Janet Labrecque and David Carl, Co-chairs, to plan a process by which a strategic plan for ACPE could be formulated. The goal is to involve people at all levels in ACPE to create a strategic plan for it to reach its goals. The Committee met in January, 1999, with one designated person from each region and regional Directors together with the President, President-Elect, Interim Executive Director and Interim Office Manager.

A plan to develop the strategic plan is being recommended to the Board at this time.

NETWORKS

In the new governance revisions in 1992 Networks were added to the category of membership:

> Network member for special interest groups intended to enhance the purpose and scope of The Association For Clinical Pastoral Education, Inc., who apply to and are approved by the Board of Representatives. (By-laws. May, 1997. p. 4.)

AMERICAN SOCIETY OF MILITARY PASTORAL EDUCATION
The American Society of Military Pastoral Education (ASNPE) exists to be supportive, interpretative and affirming for accredited Clinical Pastoral Education in all branches of the United States Military. Membership is open to all persons who desire to support the mission of CPE in the armed forces. It meets annually at the ACPE Conference. We organized about 15 years ago to say to the Army Chief of Chaplains that CPE was important in developing a corps of professional chaplains. Emory Cowen, John Teer and Dick Dennison were the pioneers in this effort. At one time there were 21 CPE centers at Army posts, but with different chiefs and economics that figure has

dropped to four. The Walter Reed program is currently training Air Force and Navy chaplains as well as Army students. (Kahrs Towley, C. March 20, 2000. Personal Communication.)

BUDDHIST
The Buddhist Chaplaincy Network was created in 1998, when Madeline Ko-I Bastis became the first Soto Zen priest to become a Board-certified chaplain. It has a four fold aim: 1) to provide a forum where Buddhist practitioners engaged in Interfaith chaplaincy can share ideas and experiences; 2) to provide information to those Buddhists wishing to pursue chaplaincy as an occupation; 3) to serve as a resource for those with questions about Buddhist chaplains; and 4) to consult with and make recommendations on standards for certification of Buddhist chaplains.

In response to the writer's question, Mike Monnett, the current Chair, explained that they also want to compile a list of ACPE programs that accept Buddhists into their programs. Mike reports:

> All of us who have been through the CPE process have found it to be an invaluable experience in shaping ourselves and our ministry, making us better able to serve sentient beings. A further reason is that we want to find out where a Buddhist would be accepted in a Supervisor In Training status. At the moment no one in the Buddhist community is actively seeking supervisory training and we do not know which program would admit a Buddhist into a year program. (Monnet, M. February 29 & March 1, 2000. Personal Communications.)

CONGREGATIONAL/COMMUNITY-BASED CPE
The mission of the Network for Congregational/Community-based CPE is to advocate for additional context in which accredited units of CPE can be offered to clergy and lay pastoral givers. It sponsors a special event at Annual Conferences with forty attending the 1999 meeting. It was a panel discussion of different ways of conducting these programs. Robert Nace, Pastor at the UCC Church at Greenville, Pennsylvania, developed the longest parish-based CPE program and was one of the early leaders in this arena. George Fitzgerald convened it until five years ago while John Galloway has convened the group for the past five years. Robert P. Rogers, Jr., is the new convenor. (Galloway, J. March 20, 2000. Personal Communication.)

GAY/LESBIAN
This Network exists to aid the Association for Clinical Pastoral Education and its members in welcoming and utilizing the gifts and graces of all its members, regardless of sexual orientation.

In 1979, four persons (three men and a woman) gathered for the first meeting of the ACPE Gay and Lesbian Caucus. Over twenty years, the caucus, now known as the Gay And Lesbian Network, has made great progress in claiming the gifts of lesbian and gay people within ACPE. Two of the original co-founders, Jim Corrigan and Jo Clare Wilson, served as co-chairs of the Network up until 1998, when Robert Petite and Elizabeth Stroop became co-convenors. It has sought the support of non-gay people within ACPE and many straight people remain active members and supporters. The Network sponsors a hospitality evening during the annual conference open to gay, lesbian and bi-sexual people only, and a business meeting where all members and all interested persons are invited to attend. It has three functions, Advocacy, Support and Education, which are spelled out on the ACPE Network website. (Petite, R. March 7, 2000. Personal Communication.)

HISTORY
John Thomas is the current convenor. It was born out of the North Central Region's History and Research Committee when Mary Saco thought that others in ACPE might like to participate. One meeting was held which drew four people. An announcement and invitation in the ACPE News to join the group resulted in no responses. The next attempt was to have a History Supplement as an addition to the RSN NEWSLETTER and to increase the RSN dues. That has been accomplished and has been included in the four issues in 1999.

Currently, the History Coordinator convenes the regional history representatives together just prior to the Annual Conference and as a History Network at the time of the Network meetings. The idea to produce a History Booklet for the 75th Anniversary came out of this group. Its future is uncertain and probably depends upon the next History Coordinator to continue the regional history representatives' meetings pattern.

INTERNATIONAL NETWORK
This network began with a conversation between Serge Castigliano and John deVelder in 1996 in Buffalo. Serge had served for many years on the ACPE International Committee and was its liaison to the International Congress of Pastoral

Care and Counseling. John agreed to organize the Network and serve as its convenor.

The first gathering of the network took place at the 1997 Conference in Orlando, Florida. A pre-conference meeting at the 1998 Conference in Portland drew over 50 people. Many international students were present, and heard some their "cultural" stories. This helped the supervisors present become more sensitive to issues of culture in their supervision. Howard Clinebell gave a keynote address and received the First International Pastoral Care Award.

In 1999, a second preconference event met in Albuquerque, New Mexico, where John Patton and Homer Jernigan gave keynotes. Another group of CPE students told their "cultural stories" of their journey in CPE. John Patton received the International Award for 1999. The planners learned the value of getting the international students together before the plenary sessions so that they got to know each other, develop a sense of belonging and cohesion during the conferences, and contribute to ACPE becoming more culturally competent in its educational mission. (deVelder, J. March 14, 2000. Personal Communication.)

PEACE
The Peace network of ACPE consists primarily of the members of ACPE who are also members of the Pastoral Care Network For Social Responsibility. In 1983, Howard Clinebell and others in AAPC had just created a Pastoral Counselor's Network for Social Responsibility patterned after the Physicians for Social Responsibility. Both official and unofficial representatives from the other cognate groups met at the 1984 ACPE Conference in Chicago and organized the Pastoral Care Network for Social Responsibility. John Thomas was the first Chair. Other groups have joined since then. This effort was in response to the Cold War and the growing danger of the nuclear threat to the world. The PCNSR is now the North American section of the International Pastoral Care Network For Social Responsibility (1991).

Sherron Hughes-Tremper has chaired the PCNSR for a number of years. It meets one evening at each Annual Conference, and sponsors a Peace walk and a simple dinner at each of the conferences. In recent years, it has broadened its concerns to add Earth Keeping. In the past ten years, Peace Walks have visited inner-city programs in the host cities. They have focused on visiting programs which seek to alleviate hunger, homelessness, places of social disease, and where peace is in short supply. Reports of peacemaking events and presentations are made by the hosting group and outside speakers and members. Two memorable ones were given by David Duncombe on "From Yale to Jail" concerning the weapons train in California. The other was by Sherron Hughes-Tremper on the Chaplaincy Response to the tragic bombing at Oklahoma City.

PUBLIC ISSUES
Myron Ebersole's 1984 request for a standing Committee on Public Issues was handled by the Board's asking the President to create a Task Force on Public Issues. It would study the possible role of ACPE in the area of Social Ethics and to report to the Board and the General Assembly. The Task Force's recommendation to the creation of a Committee on Public Issues was adopted. The Committee later on secured changes in the Standards that ask students to look also at the social forces operating in the lives of their clients, parishioners and patients.

CPE has always been comfortable in dealing with personal issues. So many individual problems are created or aggravated by larger forces and structures in society. Without efforts to change systems, pastoral care and counseling only puts Band-Aids on individuals, rather than also addressing the structures of society.

The Public Issues Network broadened to focus on CPE and social issues and problems in the inner city issues in recent years. But its small membership was reported to have "burned out" and there is no meeting planned at the 2000 Conference.

RACIAL, ETHNIC, MULTICULTURAL
Please see page 54 for more details.

RESEARCH
The purpose of the Network remains: To foster interest in the doing of pastoral research and to enable the exchange of ideas and resources for pastoral research through:
a. Publication of the Research Network Newsletter;
b. Sponsorship of Network gatherings and workshops;
c. Conferring of annual awards for outstanding researchers and research centers.

Paul Derrickson edited the Network's Newsletter in the early years, followed by Margaret Hover as Convenor, with Anne

Sutherland as Editor. Joseph Tamborini Czolgosz took over as Convenor in 1997. (Czolgosz, J. March 3, 2000. Personal Communication.)

RETIRED SUPERVISORS
Len Cedarleaf convened Emeritus and retired Supervisors at the Houston Conference in 1989, and agreed to send out a Newsletter to Emeritus and retired Supervisors. Summer 1990 was the first issue and contained a summary of brief activities of members, plus an address list of ninety-nine persons.

Due to Cedarleaf's illness, John Thomas guest-edited Vol. II of the Newsletter in 1992. Beginning in 1993 with Vol. 3, Thomas has been the Editor, publishing four issues each year. Convenor Keith Keidel offers his regular Reflections. The Newsletter primarily includes quotes from news items sent in by the members, and occasional articles by members. The group officially met at the Oakland conference in 1992 with Bob Nace serving as Chair and John Thomas as Co-Chair. Keith Keidel became the Chair/convenor the following year. It has met prior to each Annual Conference since then, with an attendance of between ten and thirty persons, depending upon site of the conference.

Currently there are about 180 retired members. Dues are now $15.00, after a $5.00 raise to pay for the additional four- to eight-page History Supplement. About 100 members pay dues and many of them contribute extra oo that every one of the 180 receives the Newsletter. The Newsletter also goes gratis to the Board, Regional Chairs, Directors and Chairs of Commissions and Committees. Many retired Supervisors do occasional supervision or serve as consultants to ongoing programs.

The Retired Supervisors' Network received the recommendation from the History Network (regional history representatives) to produce a twenty-five year History of ACPE, 1975-2000, to be presented to the registrants at the 75th CPE Anniversary Conference in May, 2000. They agreed to produce it and a campaign among the Retired Supervisors raised nearly $6,500.00 toward their goal of $7,500.00 to provide this history and other projects for the 75th Anniversary.
A "Fall Conference" was held, through the efforts of past President James Gebhart, in November, 1999, at the Thompson Center outside of St. Louis. More than forty attended, including many retired Supervisors, some spouses and some active senior supervisors. The non-structured conference highlights

included a recounting of the ways that CPE had been a blessing for them before, during and after the process of becoming Supervisors.

VETERANS AFFAIRS CPE NETWORK
This Network consists of CPE Supervisors employed by the Veterans Health Administration of the Department of Veterans Affairs. It has been meeting at ACPE Conferences since the 1960's when the VA first employed supervisors. The VA programs were initiated by the Medical Directors of the hospitals! Among the early chaplains were Thomas M. Babington, who developed ACPE programs in four different VA hospitals, and Hugh A. Maddry, Jr., who developed programs in three VA Hospitals. Carlton L. Young and Robert Dollar were among some of the other early ACPE supervisors in the Veterans Hospitals. There are now twenty-one accredited centers with ten more hospitals hosting satellite programs from other ACPE centers. There are another four centers currently looking for supervisors to develop programs. The Deputy Director is Hugh Maddry, Jr., and the convenor of the Network is Keith A. Ethridge, his associate. They formally organized as a Network in 1996. (Ethridge, K. March 20, 2000. Personal Communication.)

INTEREST GROUPS
The following groups are not networks but request meeting space at the 2000 Annual Conference: Older Adult Ministry, Clinical Members (meet as Advisory Council), Columbia HCA Chaplains and Women Professionals and Womanhood group.

ACPE AND DISASTER RELIEF

Arthur Schmidt, one of the early pioneers in this area, has provided this account of Supervisors' and ACPE's activity in utilizing their learning in the face of several types of disasters. (Schmidt, A., Jr. March 17, 2000. Personal Communication.)

> In the early 1970's, several ACPE Supervisors were involved in responding to local disasters. Among them were Vaughn Michaels, Glen Calkins, Al Embry, and others. As the ACPE Development Committee became aware of their work, the Committee considered how the ACPE could make a contribution to disaster response by training its members to be of particular help. Several times workshops were planned but the registrations did

not indicate enough interest to actually offer the workshops.

In 1980, Mt. St. Helen in Washington State erupted and Art Schmidt was asked by the Washington State Association of Churches to provide workshops for clergy and mental health workers. At that time he was a member of the ACPE Development Committee, and he took his work back to the committee and new interest was kindled. A task force of Al Embry, Vaughn Michael and Art Schmidt was formed and brought its first report to the House of Delegates' Meeting in Estes Park, Colorado in 1981. For several years this task force continued its work, and made connections with Church World Service (CWS), the domestic disaster response arm of the World Council of Churches. Several times, CWS called on the Task Force to send individuals to help in natural disasters.

As governance forms changed in the ACPE, the task force was made a network and continued to meet in connection with the national ACPE meeting. Supervisors and clinical members joined the network, and meetings focused on sharing experiences and giving members an opportunity to debrief while the others learned from their experiences.

Over the years, our members have been involved in recovery efforts from hurricanes, tornados, earthquakes, volcanoes, fires, floods, prison riots, and most dramatic in recent memory, the Oklahoma City bombings.

Several members have done some important writing about their learning, including, but not limited to Vaughn, Ken Blank, and Glen Calkins. Much of what has been written has appeared in the Journal of Pastoral Care or publications specific to various denominations. Many workshops have been conducted for community clergy, mental health groups, and others. While the influence has likely not been well documented, the contribution has been significant.

One thing that was learned along the way is that, like our educational philosophy would suggest, readiness for learning occurs after the incident. When applied to disaster response opportunities, many (who had experienced or were experiencing a disaster) were ready for an opportunity to examine their experience and learn from it.

In the late 1990's, a new opportunity presented. In 1996, Congress, after interviewing many family members of airline crash victims, passed legislation that mandated that airlines develop methods to care for the families of victims. The National Transportation Safety Board (NTSB) was given overall responsibility for responding to airline disaster. The NTSB was expected to select a non-profit organization to care for the families, and the American Red Cross (ARC) was selected. Congress mandated that a memorial service for victims take place, and the ARC had historically avoided any identification with organized religion as a way of making their help available to the many in a pluralistic society.

Some of the airlines contacted the ACPE to offer this part of the care, and the College of Chaplains contacted the ARC and offered help. As these parallel developments became known, a task force was commissioned to make plans to fill this need. The task force was composed of one member of the ACPE (Art Schmidt), one from the (newly-formed) Association of Professional Chaplains (Greg Bodin), and one from the National Association of Catholic Chaplains (Terry Becker).

These three, working with the ARC, developed methodology for the spiritual care of airline disaster victims and a training program to equip others to help. Since the inception of this effort, the National Association of Jewish Chaplains and the International Congress of Police Chaplains have been included.

To date, about 140 persons have been trained to respond with the ARC Air Incident Response Team to the site of an air disaster. A team of eight is on call every month, and they are expected to be ready to leave for a disaster site within four hours of notification. The task of the team is to recruit, train, and supervise local clergy to offer appropriate care to the victims' family or the survivors, including a memorial service as provided by Congress.

Three airline disasters have been attended by our Spiritual Response Care Team (SAIR) as well as one rail disaster.

COLLEGE OF PASTORAL SUPERVISION AND PSYCHOTHERAPY (CPSP)

In his 1975 address, Robert Powell asked the question, *Whatever happened to the development of a critical tradition within CPE?* One of the answers was found in the "UNDERGROUND REPORT" with the scripture: "...not peace but a sword..." Ray Lawrence began publishing the UNDERGROUND in 1987, following the Melbourne International conference. Early issues consisted almost entirely of letters from ACPE Supervisors debating ACPE policies. The UNDERGROUND struck a chord in the hearts of some members of each organization. Its masthead contained an impressive list of ACPE leaders as members of its Advisory Panel. It is now published as Contra Mundum with the current Vol. 12. Ray Lawrence has been publishing it since 1989. He also serves as the General Secretary of CPSP, but UR/CM and CPSP are separate. At the ACPE conference in Houston in 1989, several talked about a new organization. CPSP was founded in Roanoke, March 17, 1990, by fifteen AAPC- and ACPE certified persons who covenanted together and wrote a Covenant. This covenant is a key to understanding their organization. As Raymond Lawrence remembers it:

> Power and authority was vested almost entirely in regional small groups in CCT and in the ACPE, too, in the early years of its life... After the merger in the late '60s, the clinical pastoral movement evolved ever so subtly into a more corporate model. The balance of power and authority shifted from the grass roots to the central office and national commissions. Regions enlarged their memberships, and the previously shared life of small groups vanished, except at the training level. The consequence was the loss both of the on-going critical dimension and the caring dimension, and the loss was disastrous... A collateral consequence of the drift toward the corporate model was the gradual disappearance of the idiosyncratic, one–of-a kind pastoral counselor and clinical supervisor. (Lawrence, R. May, 1999. CPSP Pastoral Report. No. 15. p. 4-5.)

Ken Blank reports:

> CPSP is an attempt to recombine Love and Power in the same persons. I believe combining them once again is what really counts. (Blank, K. March 8, 2000. Personal Communication.)

The locus of power in CPS lies in the Chapter, a small group of pastoral psychotherapists and CPE supervisors who covenant together and know each other.

> The Chapter is the single most effective antidote to a corporate, pyramidal, hierarchical system. Virtually all power and authority rests in small grass roots communities. Chapters can do almost anything, and some have. (Lawrence, R. 1999. p. 4.)

In addition to Chapters, they have the Governing Council, which consists of permanent members and representatives from each Chapter. (CPSP Current Membership Brochure)

Ken Blank, the current President of CPSP, (also current Chair of SWRACPE) reports on the present status:

> There are approximately eighty CPSP Diplomates. Over fifty of them are dually certified by ACPE and CPSC. There are fourteen free-standing CPSP programs, two of which teach psychotherapy but are not also certified by AAPC. Twelve are free standing CPSP training programs but they are not certified by ACPE, only by CPSP. The other centers, like ours in Oklahoma, have both programs and everyone gets credit from both. I think only one or two Centers ask the student to choose and if one wants ACPE, you are asked to pay the additional fees for credit. Many Centers have ACPE and CPSP but since we do not have a national registry of credit for training, then I am unsure what each Center is doing. We are beginning a national record keeping process this spring, which will help us. (Blank, K. March 2, 2000. Personal Communication.)

The leaders are beginning to face the problem of record keeping as centers close or hospitals go out of business. Some critics like the philosophy and goals but do not like the chapters to have the authority to certify. CPSP diplomate status can either be in CPE or as Pastoral Psychotherapists. But without additional certification by CPSP, they are not transferable to each other. CPSP is also now certifying "Pastoral Psychotherapists" in addition to Diplomates. What CPSP currently is, as seen by this writer, is a network of chapters with a Tavistock-type annual meeting of the group as a whole. CPSP, because of its size, can more easily function that way.

Both CCT and IPC also started out as small groups. After all, in 1948 only about fifteen supervisors attended the CCT Supervisors' conference at the Perkiomen Inn, Schwenksville, Pennsylvania. A joint meeting there with the Institute for Pastoral Care Supervisors in 1949 only totaled about thirty supervisors. (This writer was present at each.) Size makes a tremendous difference once one gets above forty or fifty members. It is a real advantage for them that some CPSP Diplomates remain within the ACPE and AAPC organizations. CPSP takes advantage of the status of these organizations. There is some tension when a supervisor is relating to two organizations, and it raises questions among supervisors outside the CPSP program.

The Council for Clinical Training only had about sisty centers at the time of the merger, but it also had a Board of Directors which had to approve the recommendations made at the annual supervisors' general meetings.

STRATEGIC PLANNING

In 1998, The Board authorized the creation of a Strategic Planning Coordinating Committee with Janet Labreque and David Carl as Co-chairs. Its task was to design a process whereby a Strategic Plan could be developed which would involve all levels of the organization in setting goals and developing the means to accomplish them. The Committee consisted of regional Directors, another designated representative from each region, the President, President-elect, the interim Executive Director, and the interim Office Manager. The plan on how to do this is now in the process of unfolding.

SUMMARY, CONCLUSIONS AND THE FUTURE

Al Lumpkin, in his article, *Clinical Pastoral Education: Coming of Age* (1999. JHCC. Vol. 9. No. 1-2. p. 97), raises the essential question, *Will this movement endure deeply into the twenty-first century?*

"Learning from Living Human Documents" was a unique concept for theological seminaries in 1925. The early CPE movement owed much to fields other than theology. Dr. Boisen had been influenced by contemporary trends in education, social sciences, psychology and psychiatry before he had his psychotic break and hospitalization.

Supervisors following Dr. Boisen continued to learn much from the professional staffs in both general and psychiatric hospitals in which they worked. Among the many influences was Cabot's Clinical Pathology Conferences and his creation of the Professional Social Worker role. New understandings of the human body were gained through Leland Hinsie's *The Person in The Body*, Hoskins' *The Tides Of Life* and Walter Canon's *Wisdom of The Body*. In psychology, William James' *Varieties of Religious Experience,* Freud's *Collected Papers*, his *Interpretation of Dreams,* and his concept of the unconscious and repression were revolutionary! William Alanson White, Harry Stack Sullivan and the Washington School of Psychiatry, and the journal PSYCHIATRY were in the forefront of psychiatric thinking. Wilhelm Reich's *Character Analysis*, Carl Roger's *Client-Centered Therapy*, and subsequent emphases in psychology and psychiatry influenced the early supervisors. Eckstein and Wallerstein's *Teaching and Learning Psychotherapy* helped many supervisors to distinguish between learning problems and problems about learning. The breakthroughs in the 50's and 60's in the human potential movements, National Training Lab's T groups, Fritz Perls' *Gestalt Therapy*, Eric Berne's book, *Games People Play*, and the newer Self-Psychology of Kohut have all affected supervision patterns. More recently the learning theorists' positions have influenced CPE supervisors. CPE was heavily influenced by non-theological sources. At the same time, there was a new ferment in theology, with the Neibuhrs, Daniel Day Williams, Paul Tillich and many others' new voices providing their own challenges to orthodox theology.

Bob Leas observed:

> A little later in the 1970's and 1980s there was a new ferment in theology and spirituality with revisionist theologians and CPE Supervisors who sought to correlate the self-understanding, traditionally a part of CPE, with basic theological premises, challenging students to link their operational (praxis) theology with their foundational (theory) theology. People like Seward Hiltner and Wayne Oates were champions for theological integrity in CPE in the 1950s and 1960s. Today, they are succeeded by Charles Gerkin, John Patton, Don Browning, Herbert Anderson, Stanley Hauerwas, Deborah Hunsinger, and the late Henri Nouwen, to name just a few.

They are joined by a number of individual supervisors who have desired to recover ways of linking the clinical experiences of care with respective theological experiences without violating the integrity of their position nor the plurality of religious traditions and faith groups that have emerged in the past quarter century. (Leas, R. March 2, 2000. Personal Communication.)

CPE supervisors with one foot in theology and the other in both humanistic psychology and psychoanalytic tradition developed something quite unique, and perhaps inconsistent, especially in their use of the peer group for both clinical pastoral education and process group work. Joan Hemenway reminds us that *the CPE work with individual students has largely been influenced by the psychoanalytic tradition and that its process-group work has been primarily influenced by the humanistic psychology tradition.* (Hemenway, J. 1996. Introduction.)

CPE students learned from their ministry visits with patients and clients, from their relationships in the institutional staffs, in their group life, and lastly with their supervisor(s). Some supervisors asked their students in their final evaluations to write about their relationships with the patients, the professional and non-professional staff members, their student peer group members and the supervisor(s). At one institution in the 1970's and early 80's, psychologists and social workers who participated in CPE students' final evaluations (at the request of the students) were envious of the levels of self-awareness and the depths of learning reported in these group evaluation sessions. They wished that their own professional training programs had been this rich for them. (Thomas, J. 1980. Journal of Supervision and Training In Ministry.)

What was and is unique about the CPE experience was not that CPE had created a new model, but that it had blended together in the person of the Supervisor a unique individual who was willing to live on 'the boundaries." The Supervisor held the claims of theological insights and modern scientific develop-ments in tension. The Supervisor was not only living on the boundaries but she/he was willing to invite students into the ministry area and to risk learning together. The Supervisor, however, was usually not the quarterback of the professional team. CPE supervisors and their students were members of a 'team,' in contrast to the parish Pastor who was the nominal leader. This dimension of the CPE educational experience has not been fully evaluated or documented.

In addition to the educational experiences CPE has provided for thousands of clergy, seminarians, military and civilian chaplains in the last 75 years, it has changed the health and welfare institutions of the United States with chaplaincy, pastoral care, spiritual care departments. The chaplains and the supervisors who have trained them since the 1940's have developed pastoral care skills in ministering to hospital patients with every conceivable diagnosis. They have brought much-needed skills to the ministry to the terminally ill and to their bereaved family members.

We forget that chaplaincy training just didn't happen, that the rise of the several chaplaincy organizations and their certification processes owe greatly to the many supervisors who were among the founders of such organizations as the College of Chaplains (1946), The Association of Mental Health Clergy (1948), etc.

An ACPE Supervisor, Edward F. Dobihal, Jr., journeyed to England in 1971 to study the Hospice Movement and was instrumental in the founding of the first Hospice in New Haven. Two hospital chaplains, one a Supervisor and the other to become one, Rev. Carl Nighswonger and Rev. Herman Cook, were pioneers along with Dr. Elizabeth Kubler Ross at the University of Chicago Hospitals in the development of the focus on "Death and Dying" in the late 1960's and early 1970's.

Hospital Staff, physicians, surgeons, specialists in every field, nurses, therapists of all descriptions, in hospitals with CPE programs have contributed to those programs, and also have been the beneficiaries of that close collaboration for the welfare of the patients. The impact of such close interaction in many institutions has also led to a closer cooperation with the medical care specialists in the community.

Another often unrealized benefit has been for the students of the other disciplines in the hospital who have learned of the contributions religious faith makes to sick and hospitalized persons.

The list goes on and on of those who have benefited from this modern day approach to health and healing. These benefits all relate back to a clergyman who had a psychotic break in 1920 and the movement he founded, "studying the living human document."

Seminary faculties and their curricula have been significantly changed, not just by courses in Pastoral Care and Counseling, but also by the focus on the person in ministry. Denominations have had their attention called to the pastoral needs of parishioners, both in congregations and in the health and welfare institutions of our country. They have also been helped to focus on the need for the care and feeding of pastors through this movement.

Another often unrealized benefit is the rise of ecumenism due to the composition of student groups composed of students from widely differing religious backgrounds and traditions. Since the earliest years, students gathered in small groups with those of other denominations and faith traditions and became friends with those of differing religious traditions. While CPE does not deserve the full credit for this development, other organizations have been working at it. Some credit also belongs to the military chaplaincies of the armed forces where clergy of widely differing backgrounds learn to live and work together.

Another significant contribution has been to improving the ministry of the laity. The growing interest in lay training provided for thousands of persons by such groups as those described by Dr. Ronald Sutherland of Houston in the 1999 Journal of Health Care Chaplaincy is a tribute both to the success of the CPE movement, and also to Dr. Sutherland's skills in making the heart of CPE training available to the wider public. The Stephens Series is another one of the many programs for training laity.

The rise of the Parish Nurse as a profession and its growing acceptance by congregations of major denominations is a tribute to the skill of the late Dr. Granger Westberg and his CPE background. Many ACPE supervisors have provided training for this new form of lay ministry. The increasing provision of skills for training in the field of lay ministry by both supervisors and parish clergy with CPE backgrounds can be viewed as a subsidiary benefit. It is also an impressive achievement of the CPE movement. This is an effective answer to Dr. Powell's and Dr. Ogelsby's concerns twenty-five years ago about lay caregivers.

The individual ministry experiences and the peer group relationships are, of course, no longer unique to CPE. These can be now provided in field education settings where the learner can reflect on pastoral ministry experiences in peer group learning within the seminary walls. Two seminaries have even been accredited as ACPE centers! Whereas initially pastoral-counseling training was a part of CPE, now it is provided in AAPC-accredited Pastoral Counseling Training Centers and in university-based Ph.D. Counseling programs. A number of clergy are taking that route instead of the AAPC training and certification program.

As the culture has become more interested in "Spiritual Health" and "Spiritual Healing" old/new professions of healers are developing, including those of spiritual directors, grief counselors, etc.

Bob Leas has reminded the writer that there is an entirely new development with the internet and cybernetics and also how they will affect health care, ...*and it poses vast implications in the way that we deliver pastoral care education in the future in conjunction with seminary programs and our centers.* (Leas, R. February 21, 2000. Personal Communication.) Whether or not the new technology will impact the center and ACPE Programs, outreach and budgets, and in which direction remains to be seen.

The problem of funding chaplaincy programs is of great concern not only to the ACPE but to the several chaplaincy service organizations and hospitals. The recent issue of the Journal of Health Care Chaplaincy was devoted to this issue and one possible solution: Contract Chaplaincy Arrangements. The Health Care Chaplaincy in New York City is the most successful example. It combines chaplaincy service, clinical pastoral education and research in one organization. But, by means of contracts with a dozen or more different organizations, it provides chaplaincy and ACPE programs to a dozen different institutions.

The merger of hospital systems and pastoral care and ACPE programs, e.g. Advocate Health Care, combining the Evangelical and Lutheran organizations in the Chicago area is another direction. Still another development is the Alexian Brothers Health System with ACPE programs across state lines. The system carries the accreditation. The Samaritan system of Retirement Homes is yet another.

ACPE-accredited centers depend upon their support from the institutions which employ the supervisors, and that is the reason that it is so heavily dependent upon the health care institutions which require pastoral care for their patients and residents. In a few centers, successful efforts have succeeded in developing endowment funds for the programs, e.g. St. Luke's Hospital, Milwaukee, Wisconsin, where Harvey Berg, Supervisor and Department Head for many years, has developed the " Aurora Health Care, Metro Region Pastoral Care Endowment."

Harvey reported:

> We have raised nearly $4,300,000.00 to provide funding for our entire pastoral care program if necessary, but presently "to educate clergy, parish nurses, and lay pastoral caregivers of all faiths to provide spiritual comfort during times of pain and grief." It has been a most gratifying endeavor... We will only use the interest generated... A surprising learning for me has been the gratitude expressed to me by the donors for simply inviting them to be a part of our dream. (Berg, H. March 20, 2000. Personal Communication.)

The late Benjamin Patrick and his wife left over $1,000,000 to the Reynolds Pastoral Care Center at Hillcrest Medical Center, Tulsa, Oklahoma, where he had served for many years. The late Charles Teel and his wife left properties sold for $250,000.00 to fund the "Charles and Alma Teel Endowment For Clinical Pastoral Education" at Loma Linda, California. The Presbyterian Hospital, Dallas, received a $100,000.00 endowment from a physician couple to honor of their retiring Chaplain, David Erb. It often takes a long-time ministry and wealthy individuals, or persons with access to such persons and foundations for such projects. The ACPE merger was speeded up through the generosity of the W. Clement and Jessie Stone Foundation and the same Foundation assisted the Journal of Pastoral Care. The Kresge Foundation challenge grant and ACPE's response made possible the early retirement of the mortgage on our present Decatur office condominiums.

Financial support for ACPE is a requirement for its survival as an organization! Only $20,000.00 of the interest from its current endowment fund is used to fund grants for innovative programs. The balance of interest and value increase remains in the fund. ACPE is heavily dependent for its fees to support the day to day and year to year expenses and upon the local centers to pay for attendance of its certified supervisors at regional and annual conferences. Whether the new modes of communication will reduce the need for such conferences and thus the costs, is still open.

The late Dayton and Margaret Van Deusen left over $100,000.00 in their will to the ACPE Endowment Fund. It would only take a $10,000,000.00 endowment to cover the annual costs of the ACPE as an organization.

Perhaps ACPE needs a Development Officer?

Finances aside, where does this leave CPE? As long as people are willing to seek meanings in their lives and continue to respond to the Transcendent, CPE will continue to exist. As long as it can provide a place for personal growth and transformation in the process of learning pastoral care skills and continuing education for the clergy, it will be needed. Whether or not the ACPE as an organization will be here in twenty-five years depends upon factors beyond the control of ACPE.

It is a highly expensive form of education with a very low supervisor to student ratio of 1 to 6 or 7. It can be justified in non-religious settings by the pastoral services which are provided. Its venues may well change.

CPE has had a symbiotic relationship with hospitals and other therapeutic institutions since its beginnings. As long as chaplaincy services are needed in such institutions, CPE will continue to find places in some of them. The development of other types of institutions and home health care are already changing the census figures of modern hospitals. The aging of our population is already producing more problems for our health care system. Retirement housing, community-based residential facilities (CBRF), and rehabilitation centers are rapidly increasing. The "end of life" care, increasing numbers of free-standing hospice care programs and home health care agencies and services, even in retirement centers, require skilled pastoral care and well-trained supervisors. CPE programs for providing the pastoral care to the elderly and training the next generation of pastoral caregivers, both clergy and lay, will increase.

To answer Rev. Al Lumpkin's question at the beginning of this chapter is only partly for us. It depends what we are leaving. But whatever happens, this movement and this organization have made waves of its own, despite its failures and inadequacies, influencing the future. The hope is that it will continue to find new ways of serving God and humankind.

BIBLIOGRAPHY

Abstracts of Research in Pastoral Care and Counseling. (1971-1999).

ACPE By-laws. (1980, 1983, 1991, 1992, 1995, 1967, 1997).

ACPE Constitution and By-laws. (1967).

ACPE–CCT–IPC–LCC Newsletter. (Jan., April, May, June, July, Aug., Sep., Oct., Nov., Dec., 1967).

ACPE Newsletter. (1967). Vol. 1. No. 1–9.

ACPE Newsletter. (1968). Vol. 1. No. 10-12.

ACPE News. (1967-1999). Vol. II, No. 1-Vol. XXXII, No. 6.

ACPE News. (January-February, 2000). Vol. 1.

ACPE Directory of Accredited Clinical Pastoral. (1975).

ACPE Accredited Training Centers and Member Seminaries Listed by Regions, Education Centers and Member Seminaries. (1968 to 1999/2000).

ACPE Directory.

Boisen, A. (1936). The Exploration Of The Inner World. Harpers: New York, NY.

Boisen, A. (1955) Religion In Crisis and Custom. Harpers: New York, NY.

Boisen, A. (1960). Out of The Depths. Harpers: New York, NY.

Buford, P. (1997). The Lost Traditions of Women Pastoral Caregivers From 1925-1967: A "Dangerous Memory." (Th.D. Thesis). Columbia Theological Seminary: Decatur, GA.

Contract Pastoral Care and Education: The Trend of the Future. (1999). Journal of Health Care Chaplaincy (Special Issue). Vol. 9, No. 1-2.

Council for Clinical Training Annual Catalogue: Silver Anniversary. (1925-1950).

Council for Clinical Trianing Annual Catalogue. (1948-1949).

Gerkin, C. (1984). The Living Human Document. Abingdon: Nashville, TN.

Eckstein, R. and Wallerstein, R. (1958). The Teaching and Learning of Psychotherapy. International Universities Press: New York, NY.

Fukuyama, F. (May, 1999). The Great Disruption: Human Nature and the Reconstitution of The Social Order. The Atlantic Monthly. p. 55.

Hammett, H. (June, 1975). The Historical Context of The Origins of CPE. The Journal of Pastoral Care. Vol. XXIX, No. 2.

Hammett, J. (June, 1975). A Second Drink at the Well: Theological and Philosophical Context of CPE Origins. The Journal of Pastoral Care. Vol. XXIX, No. 2.

Hutchinson, R. (1999). *Chaplain At Sea, Holding On To Values In A Changing Time.* Navy Chaplain Found.: Arlington, VA.

Journal of Healthcare Chaplaincy. (1999). Vol. 1 & 2.

Journal of Supervision and Training In Ministry. (1980).

Kuether, F. (March, 1953) *Pastoral Psychology, The Council for training.* Pastoral Psychology In The East. Vol. 4, No. 36.

Lawrence, R., Jr. (May, 1999). *CPSP Pastoral Report.* Special Report from the CPSP General Secretary. No. 15.

Lumpkin, A. (1999). *USDE Concerns.* (Videotape).

Lumpkin, A. (1999). Journal of Health Care Chaplaincy. Vol. 9, No.1-2.

Oglesby, W., Jr. (1975). *Heritage and Commitment: CPE in the Second Half Of The Century.* ACPE Conference Proceedings. p. 88.

Powell, R. (1975). *Anton T. Boisen.* AMHC.

Powell, R (1975). 1975 ACPE Conference Proceedings.

Powell, R. (March 18, 1999). Whatever Happened to "CPE:" Clinical Pastoral Education? (Unpublished paper). Ninth Plenary Meeting of CPSP.

Rasuchenbush, W. (1906). Christianity and Crisis. New York, NY. p. 366-372.

Schlesinger, A., Jr. (December, 1999). *The Glorious and The Damned.* AARP Bulletin.

Schools of Pastoral Care Affiliated With the Institute of Pastoral Care, Directory of Programs. (1967).

Student A. (Spring, 1951). Clinical Pastoral Education As a Religious Experience. Journal of Pastoral Care. Vol. 5, No. 1. p. 33.

The NACC: A Twenty-Year History. (August, 1985). The National Association of Catholic Chaplains (Special Publications).

Thomas, J. (1979). *Staff Participation in Final Evaluation (CPE) Seminars.* Journal of Supervision and Ministry. Vol. 2.

Thomas, J. (1999). *Supervisors' Questionnaire On "Your Evaluation of Changes in CPE."* (Unpublished Survey).

Van Wagner, C.; Hand, Q.;. and Stokes, A. (1992). *AAPC in Historical Perspective: 1963-1991.* The American Association of Pastoral Counselors.

APPENDIX I. A SUPERVISOR'S EARLY NONTHEOLOGICAL LIBRARY PRIOR TO 1960
Learning also took place from books!

Alexander, F. and French, T. (1946). Psychoanalytic Therapy. Ronald Press, New York, NY.

Boisen, A. (1936). The Exploration of The Inner World. Harpers: New York, NY.

Boisen, A. (1945, 1955). Religion in Crisis and Custom. Harpers: New York, NY.

Boisen, A. (1960). Out Of The Depths. Harpers: New York, NY.

Cabot, R. and Dicks, R. (1936). The Art of Ministering to The Sick. Macmillian: New York, NY.

Cannon, W. (1939). The Wisdom of The Body, (Revised and Enlarged Edition). WW Norton: New York, NY.

Coe, G., (1916). The Psychology of Religion. University of Chicago Press: Chicago, IL.

Eckstein and Wallerstein. (1958). Teaching and Learning Psychotherapy. Internat'l Universities Press: New York, NY.

English, S. and Pearson, G. (1945). Emotional Problems of Living. WW Norton: New York, NY.

Frankl, V. (1959). From Death Camp to Existentialism. (First Published in German in 1946). Beacon Press: Boston, MA.

Hiltner, S. (1958). A Preface to Pastoral Theology. Abingdon Press: Nashville, TN.

Hiltner, S. (1943). Religion and Health. Macmillian: New York

Hiltner, S. (1950). The Counselor In Counseling. Abingdon Press: Nashville, TN.

Hinsie, L. (1945). The Person in the Body. WW Norton: New York, NY.

Korzybski, A. (1941). Science and Sanity. (2nd Edition, International Non-Aristotelian Library). Science Press: Lancaster, PA and NewYork, NY.

Mc Neill, J. (1921). A History of The Cure of Souls. Harpers: New York, NY.

Mead, G. (1924). Mind, Self and Society. University of Chicago Press: Chicago, IL.

Menninger, K. (1938). Man Against Himself. Harcourt Brace: New York, NY.

Oates, W. (1955). Religious Factors in Mental Illness. Association Press: New York, NY.

Reich, W. (1949). Character Analysis. (3rd Enlarged Edition, Translated by Theodore P. Wolfe). Orgone Institute Press: New York, NY.

Rogers, C. (1950). Client Centered Therapy. Houghton Mifflin: Boston, MA.

Wise, C. (1942). Religion In Illness and Health. Harpers: New York, NY.

Wise, C. (1951). Pastoral Counseling, Its Theory and Practice. Harper and Brothers: New York, NY.

Young, R. (1954). The Pastor's Hospital Ministry. Broadman Press: Nashville, TN.

JOURNALS
The Journal of Clinical Pastoral Work CCT. (1948).
The Journal of Pastoral Care. (1948-1959).
Pastoral Psychology. (1950-1959).

APPENDIX II. PRESIDENTS OF ACPE

1967-1969	John I. Smith* (IPC)
1970-1971	Charles V. Gerkin (CCT)
1972-1973	Albert L. Meiburg (ACP Educators)
1974-1975	Henry H. Cassler* (CCT & Lutheran)
1976-1977	William B. Oglesby, Jr.* (Union Seminary, Richmod, VA)
1978-1979	J. Lennart Cedarleaf* (CCT)
1980-1981	John R. Thomas (CCT)
1982-1983	Aldine E. Anderson (CCT & Lutheran)
1984-1985	Jasper N. Keith, Jr.
1986-1987	James F. Gebhart.
1988-1989	Max R. Maguire
1990-1991	Julian L. Byrd
1992-1993	Kathy A. Turner
1994-1995	Urias H. Beverly
1996-1997	William J. Baugh
1998-1999	Jo Clare Wilson
2000-	James D. Stapleford
2000-	James L. Gibbons, President-elect

*deceased

APPENDIX III. RECIPIENTS OF THE ACPE'S DISTINGUISHED SERVICE AWARD

1980	Seward Hiltner*
1981	Carroll A. Wise*
1982	John Billinsky*
1983	Ernest E. Bruder* (Posthumously)
1984	J. Obert Kempson*
1985	Charles E. Hall, Jr.*
1986	J. Lennart Cedarleaf*
1987	Fritz Norstad*
1988	John R. Thomas
1989	Helen T. Terkelson* (Posthumously)
	P. Wesley Aitken
	Edward J. Mahnke
1990	Louis L. McGee
1991	George L. Colgin
1992	John I. Smith* (Posthumously)
1993	No award

1994	Max Maguire
	Albert L. Meiburg
1995	Henry C. Brooks
1996	William F. Nisi* (Posthumously)
1997	James L. Gibbons
1998	Edward F. Dobihal, Jr.
1999	Agnes Barry
2000	Joan E. Hemenway

*deceased

APPENDIX IV. ACPE CONFERENCE INFORMATION

1964   Joint – What Constitutes Supervision. Chicago, Oct. 13-17.

1965   Joint – Concerns: Clinical and Theological Education, Miami, Oct. 18-22.

1966   Joint – Pastoral Supervision and His Identity. Atlantic City, Oct. 17-20.

1967   ACPE Merger: New Thrusts in Clinical Education, Kansas City, Oct. 17-20.

1968   New Thrusts In Clinical Education. Chicago, Oct. 18-21.

1969   A Ministry in the 70's for A World of the 70's. Denver, Oct. 31-Nov. 1.

1970   Joint AAPC and ACPE. Boston, Nov. 10-13.

1971   Joint AAPC and ACPE, Celebration of Awareness. San Francisco, Nov. 10-13.

1972   CPE and Health Care Delivery. Houston, Oct. 15-18.

1973   Theology as Response. St. Louis, Oct. 15-22.

1974   Clinical Education: Heresy & Orthodoxy. Atlanta, Nov. 14-16.

1975   50th Anniversary Celebration. Minneapolis, Oct. 16-19.

1976   Joint CAPE-ACPE, Exploring Our Spiritual Resources. Detroit, Oct. 21-23.

1977   The Church and The Seminary. New York, Nov. 9-12.

1978   Human Ecology, Hope & Responsibility. Seattle, Nov. 8-11.

1979   To Serve The Present Age – Personal and Political Power Oct. 18-21.

1980   Theological Education In The 1980s. New Orleans, Nov. 5-7.

1981   Making and Keeping Life Human. Estes Park, Nov. 4-8.

1982   Revisioning Supervision-Embarking On A Pilgrimage. Indianapolis, Nov. 9-12.

1983   CPE: Spirituality In The Community Of Faith. Portland, ME, Oct. 11-15.

1984   1984-2001: Agendas For Education In Ministry. Chicago, Oct. 30-Nov. 2.

1985   Strangers In Our Midst. San Diego, Nov. 12-15 & Hawaii

1986   Crisis: Danger and Opportunity. Atlanta, Oct. 7-10.

1987   20th Anniversary: Caring Choices-Life, Liberty & the Pursuit... Philadelphia, Nov. 3-7.

1988   Dialogue '88. Minneapolis, Oct. 30- Nov 4.

1989   Education As Creation. Houston, Oct. 31-Nov. 4.

1990	Unity In Diversity, Diversity In Unity. Baltimore, Nov.6-11
1991	Rediscovery Of The Soul, Revaluing For The 21st Century. Breckenridge, Nov. 15-24.
1992	Silver Anniversary: Re-Shaping The Foundation. Oakland, Nov. 4-8.
1993	The Uneasy Grace of Sexuality. Louisville, Nov. 10-13.
1994	Dialogue '94. Milwaukee, May 1-4.
1995	Weaving A Vision. Providence, May 4-6.
1996	Crucible of Change. Buffalo, May 1-4.
1997	The Middle Of The Magic. Orlando, May 1-4.
1998	Joint Meeting With APC: The Merger of AMHC & COC. Portland, April 29-May 2.
1999	Blooming In The Desert. Albuquerque, April 19-May 2.
2000	75th CPE Anniversary: Where The Sacred Encounter Theology And The Arts. Arlington, May 3-7.

APPENDIX V. REGIONAL CHAIRS AND DIRECTORS BY REGIONS

Regional Directors by Regions (Information From the Annual ACPE Directories). Please notice the long tenure of some regional directors: Jasper N. Keith, Jr., at 17 years; John Whitesel, 15 years; M. Jerry Davis, John R. Thomas and E. Augustus Verdery each 12 years.

Northeast Region. (Maine, Massachusetts, New Hampshire, Rhode Island, Vermont)

1967	John Waters
1969	John I. Smith*
1978	John Higgins
1990	Scott Hinrichs
1993	Carol J. McAninch-Pritz (interim)
1994	Carl Kahrs Towley

Eastern Region. (Connecticut, Delaware, New Jersey, New York, Pennsylvania, Puerto Rico)

1967	Henry Cassler*
1973	E. Dean Bergen*
1983	Joan E. Hemenway
1990	Jeffery M. Silberman, Susan Mello, Administrative Officer
1994	E, Dean Bergen Denise Haines, Interim Administrative Officer
1997	James B. Jeffrey, Interim
2000	John J. Gleason

Mid-Atlantic. (District of Columbia, Maryland, North Carolina, Virginia, West Virginia)

| | David Gregory and P. Wesley Aitken, Regional Representatives |
| 1967 | David Gregory |

1967	Harold Yoder
1973	Fred Reid
1974	Robert Robey
1978	Maurice Briggs
1987	Jack Stearns
1995	George T. Karl
2000 (May)	Agnes Barry

Southeast Region. (Alabama, Florida, Georgia, Mississippi, South Carolina, Tennessee)

1967	J. Obert Kempson
1969	E. Augustus Verdery
1983-	Jasper N. Keith, Jr.

East Central Region. (Indiana, Kentucky, Michigan -Except Upper Peninsula, Ohio, Pennsylvania -Pittsburgh area)

1967	Robert Alexander and William Kibler, Jr., Regional Representatives
1968	John Whitesel
1984	Dennis Kenny
1990	Jo Clare Wilson
1992	Frank Ciampa

North Central Region. (Northern Illinois, Iowa, Michigan -Upper Peninsula, Minnesota, North Dakota, South Dakota, Wisconsin)

1967	John R. Thomas
1979	James Anderson
1987	Alice E. McLaughlin, Interim
1988	O.O. "Oz' Anderson
1997	Clyde Burmeister
2000 (Sep.)	Gary Sartain

South Central Region. (Colorado, Southern Illinois, Kansas, Missouri, Nebraska, Wyoming)

1968	Paul Kapp
1970	Duane Parker
1977	Jack Slaughter
1981	B. Preston Borgia
1987	Robert Pattie
1996-	Stuart Plummer

Southwest Region. (Arkansas, Louisiana, New Mexico, Oklahoma, Texas)

1967	Richard A. Donnewirth and J. Winton Gable, Regional Representatives
1968	Thomas Shannon
1969	Kenneth Pepper
1970	Thomas Cole
1979	Ronald Wilkins
1985	Donald Bratton
1990	Robert Grigsby
1996-	Deborah Whisnand

Pacific Region. (Alaska, Arizona, California, Hawaii, Idaho, Montana, Nevada, Oregon, Utah, Washington)

1967	Robert R. Dollar, Regional Representative
1968	Robert R. Dollar
1972	Elmer Laursen
1976	John M. Humphreys
1980	J. Lennart "Len" Cedarleaf
1988-	M. Jerry Davis

APPENDIX VI. CURRENT ACPE FEES FOR 2000

CPE Center Membership-Accreditation. See Weighting Scale and Explanation from $450.00 minimum to $7,500.00 maximum for 242 units previous year

CPE Cluster, System Membership-Accreditation	same as above
CPE Supervisor Membership-Certification	$300.00
Retired Supervisor (doing supervision in 2000)	$110.00
Retired Supervisor (no supervision in 2000)	$ 55.00
Inactive Supervisor	$150.00
Supervisory Candidate	$110.00
Faith Group/Agency Membership	$175.00
Annual Seminary Membership Scale	
0 - 300	$290.00
301 - 600	$400.00
600 +	$475.00
Clinical Member	$110.00
Individual Member	$ 75.00
Retired Member	$ 50.00
Student Affiliate Member	$ 50.00
Network Member (For Network, not individuals)	$ 1.00
International Affiliate Organization	$100.00
Certification Review	
For Associate Supervisor	$400.00
For CPE Supervisor	$650.00
Accreditation Review	$600.00
ACPE NEWS Advertising (Per Issue–75 pages)	$150.00
(Additional $1.00 per word over 75 words)	
Conference Registration	Changes Each Year

APPENDIX VII. SUPPORTERS OF 75th ANNIVERSARY BOOKLET, VIDEO AND BANNER

Regions: Northeast, Southeast, Eastern, North Central, South Central.

Retired Supervisors:

Abbott, Jo Boone	Aitken, Paul Wesley	Anderson, OO
Belgum, David	Bowman, George	Brown, Frank
Burmeister, Clyde	Byrd, Julian	Carpenter, Ralph

Clark, Maurice*   DeArment, Dan   Dobihal, E. F. Jr.
Duncombe, David   Ebersole, Myron
Eichorn, Herman "Ike" Futscher, Roy   Gerkin, Charles
Gilbert,Larry   Gleason, Jack   Gross, Joe
Hall, Charles E.***   Hart, Charles
Hughes-Tremper, Sherron**   Hughey, Wilbur
Hunt, Thomas   Jeffrey, James   Johnson, Art
Johnson, David   Keidel, Keith   Leas, Robert*
Lehman, Richard   Mace, Gene   Madden, Myron
Maguire, Max   Mahnke, Edward   Moyer, Frank
Nelson, Harold   Parker, Duane**   Rankin, John K.
Russell, William   Saltzgiver, L. Burns   Snorton, Teresa**
Snyder, Milton   Steele, Guy   Thomas, John R.
Thornton, Edward   Tingue, Arthur   Wadowicz, Joseph
Wilson, Jr. O.Chappell**   Wyatt, David
Wylie, James

*   Deceased, given by Harriett Clark
**   Active Supervisors
*** Deceased, given by John R. Thomas

APPENDIX VIII. PHOTO INDEX

1. Inside Front Cover. Anton T. Boisen (1876-1965).
2. Group Photo of History Network, Whose Idea it was to Publish This Text. Rear Row: O. Chappell Wilson, Jr., Robert Leas, Jerry Davis. Front Row: Myron Ebersole, John Thomas, and Ray Bailey.
3. Homer Jernigan.
4. Edward Thornton
5. Charles E. Hall
6. Joan Hemenway
7. Seward Hiltner, Seated. John Thomas, Podium (1980).
8. Carroll Wise
9. Wayne Oates, Edward Thornton, and Aldine Anderson (1983).
10. John Billinsky
11. Frederick C. Kuether
12. Malcolm & Marjorie Ballinger
13. J. Obert Kempson
14. History Panel at Chicago. Left to Right: J. Lennart Cedarleaf, Wayne Oates, John Thomas and Emil Hartl. (1984).
15. Special Study Committee. Left to Right: Robert Morris, William Johnson, Ray Otto, James Gebhart, Chair, James Gibbons, John Thomas, Robert Eades (not pictured, Robert Erickson, consultant, H. Rhea Gray).
16. Louise Long, First Woman Supervisor.
17. Installation of Kathy Turner. Left to Right: James Gebhart, Kathy Turner, Julian Byrd, Max Maguire, Jasper Keith, Aldine Anderson, and John Thomas.
18. Installation of Jo Clare Wilson (Right); Kathy Turner (Left).
19. Donald Shmauz, First ACPE Roman Catholic Supervisor.

20. George Polk.
21. Cameron Byrd.
22. Thanda Ngcobo. At San Diego. (1985).
23. Henry Brooks
24. John I. Smith and Charles E. Hall, at Dedication of Plaque at Worcester State Hospital.
25. Aldine Anderson and Duane Parker (1982 Campaign).
26. Helen Patton.
27. Russell H. Davis (Left); Urias Beverly, (Right).
28. Stuart Plummer.
29. Teresa Snorton
30. Past Presidents. Left to Right: Charles Gerkin, J. Lennart Cedarleaf, John Thomas, Aldine Anderson, Albert Meiburg, James Gebhart, and William Ogelsby.
31. Henry Cassler
32. W. Clement Stone (First ACPE Appreciation Award).
33. Past Presidents. Rear: Urias Beverly, Jo Clare Wilson, William Baugh, Duane Parker (Past Executive Director).Front: John Thomas, Max Maguire, Kathy Turner.
34. James Gibbons
35. 1987 Conference; Melbourne, Australia.

36. Public Issues Committee. Left to Right: Joan Hemenway, James Gebhart, Myron Ebersole, Robert Carlson, Arthur Schmidt.
37. Bust of Dr. Anton Boisen, by William J. Johnson, Jr.

INDEX – Proper names of those in Photographs

INDEX: Not a subject index: Proper Names Only – Supplement to page 123

Toback, Phyllis	53
Towley, Carl Kahrs	95
Vande Creek, Larry	84
Van Deusen, Dayton	112
Waff, Razz	86
Wagner, Ruth	50
Wallasky, Maxine	50
Wallerstein	106
Way, Peggy	34
Westberg, Granger	109
Whisnand, Deborah	50
White, William A.	106
Wilkins, Mary	50,52
Williams, Daniel Day	106
Wittrip, Richard	74
Young, Carlton	100

Errata

Add to Biblography: Special Study Committee Report, 1980, ACPE
Correct: 17 Sheehan, Barbara; p. 95 Towley, Carl Kahrs; p. 98 Hover, Margo